GET

MONEY SAVVY

TAKE CONTROL OF YOUR LIFE, GET OUT OF DEBT, & LIVE YOUR DREAMS

Matt Kelly

www.PersonalFinanceCoaching.com

To Cheri and Malcolm

CONTENTS

Acknowledgments

For nine years I wrote the personal finance column *Money Savvy* which appeared in the *Durango Herald*. Between 2009 and 2018, I wrote more than 100 columns. This book is a collection of 52 of my columns, curated to help you take control of your life and money, get out of debt, and live the life of your dreams.

I am deeply grateful to the staff, management, and ownership of the Durango Herald for the opportunity to share my experience of getting out of debt, taking control of my life, and living my dreams.

Matt Kelly, Personal Finance Coach

www.PersonalFinanceCoaching.com

Introduction

I wish I'd known then what I know now. Except that if I had known, I wouldn't be sharing this information with you now. What I wish I'd known is how to stop the dream thief from stealing my dreams.

It was 1989; I thought I was buying into the "American Dream." I was 23 years old when I embarked on my master's degree program. Two years later, with my newly minted Master of International Management, I was ready to live the dream. More like a life that would see my dreams stolen by a thief – debt and unconscious spending.

My lifestyle was financed by debt - student loans, credit cards, and car payments.

In the spring of 1995, I was joined in *My American Dream* by my new wife, Cheri. We were on our way. We bought a condo two blocks west of Wrigley Field in Chicago, got married, took our honeymoon, and Cheri was set to start her master's program at Northwestern University.

To buy out condo we had to pay off my $10,000 in credit card debt. We did that by selling a stock portfolio, Cheri's grandfather had built for her. Credit card debt was gone! The down payment and closing costs took the rest.

Eighteen months later, the credit card debt was back. We'd paid for some of our wedding expenses, enjoyed a nice honeymoon, overspent on restaurants and fun, and I'd had my best year ever as an entrepreneur. But I hadn't planned on taxes. I wrote an $8,000 credit card check to the IRS.

We had $18,000 in credit card debt, and Cheri was about to finish her Master's degree, which added $50,000 in student loans to my already $20,000.

We were officially broke.

Fortunately, Food and Wine magazine had ranked our Chicago neighborhood as one of the hottest in the country. We'd paid $72,000 for our condo and sold it that summer for $96,000.

At the closing, the checks were paid directly to Visa, Master Card, and Discover. The smallest was for us. We bought a larger condo in an up-and-coming neighborhood, and I declared, "Never again!" It happened again and again.

Like so many Americans Cheri and I were in a cycle of accumulating credit card debt and paying it off by rolling our credit card debt into our mortgage and declaring, "Never again!"

Without any skills or tools to change our behavior, it happened again and again…for nearly sixteen years.

I believed the lies. I believed that debt, credit cards, and car payments were tools that would allow me to live "the good life." Indeed, spending unconsciously and living in debt was giving me something I wanted – the ability to pretend that I was achieving my dreams and avoid my reality.

Our dream. Since before Cheri and I were married we had talked about taking a year off from work to travel the world.

At times, when our debts had been rolled into their mortgage, the dream seemed more likely to happen. Of course, moving debt from one place to another did not really ever pay it off; it just hid the reality of our situation.

The truth was I had stopped dreaming. It was the easiest way to stop the negative judgments of myself without having to give up my behavior and confront my choices around money. Over those 16 years, the price became too high. The pain of not living my dreams was greater than the pain of changing.

In February 2007, Cheri and I began attending the thirteen-week Financial Peace University. Over the following fifteen months, we paid off $165,000 in debt and saved $20,000. No, we didn't have huge incomes. We had received a $40,000 inheritance when my parents passed away – which we didn't use to go to Hawaii. Instead, we paid off some debt. In addition to using the $40,000 to pay off debt, we harnessed our $80,000 annual income to pay off an additional $25,000 in debt and save $20,000.

The remaining $100,000 debt payoff came from this shared dream. Realizing that paying off our home would be a key component to being able to travel around the world freely, Cheri and I decided to downsize their condo. We sold our $300,000 condo that had a $200,000 mortgage and bought a $200,000 condo using a $100,000 down payment. We liked the new smaller condo better and could foresee the day when they will embark on their journey around the world.

After having gone through the process of getting out of debt, our marriage is better, there is more ease in our life, and we are happier. And the best thing is that I found he has a passion and a gift for helping others get out of debt too.

If debt is stealing your dreams, or you have not learned to tell your money where to go instead of wondering where it went, this book is for you.

Matt Kelly

Portland, Oregon

More information about Matt's personal finance coaching practice and how he can help you take control of your life and money, get out of debt, and live your dreams can is online at

www.PersonalFinanceCoaching.com

1

Control Your Money, Reclaim Your Dreams

But life hasn't always been that way for me. In 2007, my wife and I were drowning in debt. Our credit cards were maxed out. We had $65,000 in credit card and student loan debt. Worst of all, I'd lost my dreams.

Maybe you feel like I did?

- Do you feel like you are making enough money but you aren't getting ahead?
- Do you wonder where your money goes every month?
- Do you have credit card debt that you wish you could pay off?
- Do you feel like there is always some small financial crisis to manage?
- Are your dreams of travel, adventure, or financial stability a distant memory?

If you answered "yes" to any of these questions, the next four Money Savvy columns are for you. Today, in three action steps, I'll help you start to regain control of your money and, ultimately, reclaim your dreams.

Step 1: Motivation

Get a journal or notebook. Ask yourself, "Why do I want to take control of my money?" Write down your answer, but don't stop with your first response – or your second. Keep asking "why" and keep answering. This is crucial.

By going deeper and deeper into why you want to take control of your money, you will understand your true motivations — knowing why taking control of your money is important to you will help you set a course for your future and help you create new habits and behaviors.

Step 2: Budget

In your notebook, create a budget with these four levels:

- **Necessities:** I like to call them warm, safe, and dry. They include rent/mortgage, groceries, utilities, and gas for your car.
- **Obligations:** These are debts and contractual agreements that carry consequences if they go unpaid.
- **Less than monthly expenses:** Remember Christmas? Each month, set aside money for expenses that occur only occasionally or unexpectedly.
- **Nice-to-haves:** These are small luxuries such as restaurant meals, entertainment, miscellaneous expenses, and spending money.

2

Write down how much you spend for each expense in the four categories. Now, cut your planned spending as much as you can. The money you save each month will buy back your dreams.

Step 3: Controlled spending

Start using cash to pay for your groceries and all of your small luxuries. Each time you get paid, withdraw cash; then put it in envelopes labeled with the name of each expense. Only spend the money in the envelope for its intended use. When the cash is gone, you're out of money for that category until your next payday.

Once complete, you will have told your money where it's going and be saving for future expenses each month.

Next, we'll tackle paying off your debt in 12 to 18 months.

2

DROWNING IN DEBT? GRAB THIS LIFE PRESERVER

Credit card debt can feel like drowning. I know. I've had balances of more than $25,000. I was in deep.

If you have credit card debt, you have plenty of company. Thirty-eight percent of U.S. households are carrying credit debt. The average balance is $6,885.

This level of debt can feel overwhelming. Will I ever be able to come up for air? A plan for taking control of your money and paying off that debt is just the life preserver you need.

In week 1, I gave you a method for discovering why paying off your debt is important to you, for creating a budget and for using cash for all of your discretionary spending. This is the foundation for what comes next.

To eliminate your debt, facing reality is Step 1. From the smallest balance to the largest, make a list of your credit cards. For each, note the balance and minimum payment. Add up the total. Congratulations! You've completed the first and often most difficult step.

Now that you know how much you owe, I recommend that you plan to pay it off in 12 to 18 months. Divide the total of your credit card debt by the number of months you chose. For example, if you had a balance of $6,885 and wanted to pay it off in 12 months, you need to pay your minimum payments and $574 each month.

Instead of paying more than the minimum on all of your cards, focus on the smallest balance first. The focus will create intensity and momentum. Once you pay off the smallest balance, add the minimum payment from that card to the next one on your list. Stacking the minimum payments will accelerate your progress.

How do you come up with the extra $547 you'll need each month? Here are three options:

- **Cut your spending:** Revisit your budget to eliminate spending that is less important than the reason you want to be out of debt.
- **Sell things you own:** Use this money to pay off your cards. Don't forget to consider selling things you owe debt on, too. This delivers the double benefit of paying off debt and freeing up that payment to attack your credit debt.
- **Work extra hours:** An additional 15 hours a week at $10 an hour would give you the money you need.

If you want to get out of debt quickly, coming up with extra money will probably mean a combination of cutting spending, selling stuff and working more. If the amount of extra money you need each month seems overwhelming, extend the amount of time you have given yourself to become debt-free – try 24, 30 or even 36 months.

Establish a timeline that motivates you and doesn't discourage you. Your success should build on itself. Each month, you should feel a growing momentum toward your goal.

Next, we'll address avoiding financial chaos and crisis.

3

STOP THOSE 3 A.M. MONEY WORRIES

If you're like me, money worries hit hardest in the middle of the night. Fortunately, fear and anxiety about money don't intrude on my sleep the way they once did.

Unplanned expenses used to pop into my mind like a terrible version of whack-a-mole. I'd say, "If we just had a 'normal month,' everything would be OK." The truth is, things break, go wrong, and cost money. Not being prepared was causing financial stress and chaos.

You can be prepared for upcoming expenses and stop your middle-of-the-night worries by accumulating money each month for predictable, less-than-monthly expenses such as tires, holidays, and insurance.

Name an expense of yours that can become a minor emergency if you aren't prepared for it. Let's start there.

Look ahead

With your future minor emergency in mind, estimate how much it will cost to resolve. By when will it be a problem if you don't take

7

action? These steps may require some research. Don't avoid knowing – it won't make the expense disappear. Trust me; I've tried.

Realistic budget

To calculate how much you will need to save each month, divide the cost of the expense by the number of months until it occurs. For example, if winter tires will cost $600 and you will need to buy them in six months, you'll need to be saving $100 a month.

As you make this a habit, planning for predictable less-than-monthly expenses will prevent them from becoming minor emergencies that can take months to reconcile.

Peace of mind

With the knowledge of how much you need to save each month, you will have to reprioritize your spending. Remember, it's the peace of mind and a good night's sleep that you're after, not just covering expenses. Make your peace of mind a priority.

Accumulating money

If I left the money I was saving for future expenses in my checking account, I'd be tempted to spend it. I recommend transferring that money out of your primary checking account at the end of each month into an account I call a "momentum account."

Notice I didn't call it a savings account? I don't like savings accounts. They tend to become a general fund where money has multiple purposes. It's for vacation, car repairs, dentist visits, and a wish list of other possible expenditures that you don't have the money for right now.

Open a momentum account

This month, take action. Open a checking account to serve as your momentum account. I recommend a checking account so you can use a debit card and online bill pay. You can also transfer money into to and out of the account easily.

At the end of the month, transfer the money you have allocated to preventing your minor financial emergency. This preparation will allow you to rest easy.

Next up, how to make your dreams a reality.

4

REKINDLE YOUR DREAMS GOAL BY GOAL

There are no coincidences. I sat down to write this column, turned on Pandora and Shakira's "Try Everything" from "Zootopia" started blasting.

"I won't give up.

No, I won't give in,

till I reach the end.

And then, I'll start again.

I wanna try everything.

I wanna try, even though I could fail."

Give it a listen at http://bit.ly/MoneySavvyMotivation.

In my 20s and 30s, I unwittingly traded my dreams for debt and unconscious spending. These days, I'm busy living my dreams – trying, failing, and not giving up. I can help you do the same.

Don't worry. We'll start small, so you can slowly reconnect with what you want most. After all, isn't that how we let go of our dreams – little by little until they fade from sight.

Here are three categories of dreams that can stoke your motivation:

- Immediate: something small that costs more than you have in current disposable income.
- Significant: bucket-list goals, such as a vacation or one-time purchase.
- Impactful: dreams that connect you with your deepest purpose or mission.

Immediate dreams

Ideally, fulfilling an immediate dream will take two to four months of savings. Pick an activity or purchase you've put off because it's just a little out of reach financially. Now, set aside cash each month in an envelope or special place until you hit your goal. Soon, you will be able to celebrate hitting that goal, and you'll build psychological momentum for pursuing larger ones.

Significant dreams

If you don't have a bucket list, get a journal, and list one-time experiences or purchases that will make life richer or more fulfilling. Use your imagination to recall wishes and dreams from your youth. To bring your list to life, you can create a vision board. Check out this article for guidance: http://bit.ly/HowToMakeADreamBoard.

11

These dreams will be powerful enough to guide you toward taking control of your money, paying off debt, and creating a realistic budget to save for that big goal.

Take a personal retreat

Once you are making progress toward that bucket-list goal, take a quiet three-day weekend to consider the impact you want to make on the world.

On Day 1, take a walk in nature. Awaken without an alarm clock on Day 2, then spend time journaling. After journaling, spend the day with someone or doing something that inspires you. That evening, review your journal entry to see if your impact dream has emerged. Spend Day 3 walking in nature, journaling, and planning.

Abolitionist Harriet Tubman said: "Every great dream begins with a dreamer. Always remember, you have within you the strength, the patience, and the passion to reach for the stars to change the world."

5

Nine Things A Year Of Travel Taught Me

As a personal finance coach, I warn clients that debt steals your dreams.

I've long known the power of them to guide financial choices, but now as I reflect on living one of my dreams, traveling for a year, I can see that the real impact of living out a dream is transformation, not the activities or purchases.

Here is what I learned from 13 months of living and working in San Francisco, Boston, Honolulu, and Philadelphia. My wife, Cheri, and I and our son, Malcolm, drove across the country – twice, taking numerous side trips and doing the Lonely Planet Guide's top 10 things most everywhere we went.

1. **Your commitment will be tested**. Obstacles arose before, during, and after. I was tempted to quit before starting. Along the way, I wanted to return to my comfort zone. I learned that returning could be difficult too.

13

2. **Get out of your comfort zone**. Fear and social constraints can hold me back if I choose to let them.

3. **Explore your world.** We lived like locals but explored like visitors. As a result, we saw and did things most locals never did.

4. **10,000 steps a day – good for health and soul**. Because we had only one vehicle, I did a lot of walking. To be exact, I took 3,481,540 steps, covering 1,420 miles. The opportunity to slow down, connect with my surroundings, and see new and different things each time I walk has enlivened my soul.

5. **Security comes through relationships**. Our vulnerability was met with generosity and connection. Friends and acquaintances opened their homes and community to us. Without this support, it would have been nearly impossible to take the leap of faith required to start and continue this year of travel.

6. **Find hidden gems**. Every place has a story to tell if I'm willing to see it with new eyes. I learned this through Big City Hunt, a self-led scavenger hunt designed to help you get to know your city and places you visit.

7. **Want more serenity, consider less stuff**. We never touched much of what we brought with us. When I opened our storage unit last week here in Durango, I didn't want most of what was in it. We learned to live with less. And we're happier.

8. **13 weeks, time for transformation, and play**. Cheri was working as a traveling speech therapist. Each contract was for 13 weeks, one-quarter of a year – one season. I learned that this was enough time to make a significant transformation. And 13 weeks has 26 weekend days. Nearly a month of vacation-like play.

9. **Choose adventure**. Life can be difficult, stressful, and filled with risks. Sometimes my worry makes me want to hide and play it safe. When I breathe, I know that a life of adventure comes with risks, but playing it safely comes with the certainty of a smaller, less vibrant world.

Don't let debt steal your dreams!

6

THE 'GOOD LIFE' DOESN'T INCLUDE CHASING MONEY

Is the only thing standing between you and the "good life" more money? If you believe this, you're not alone. Most of us assume money and happiness are connected. And they are, but just not as much as you may think.

When it comes to household income, the magic number is $75,000, say Princeton economist Angus Deaton and Nobel Laureate psychologist Daniel Kahneman. As people earn more money, it has a direct, positive effect on their happiness until they reach an income of $75,000 – or $18.75 per hour assuming 2,000 hours of work per year for a two-income family.

Beyond $75,000, earning more can become a futile pursuit on the hedonic treadmill, illustrated by this quote by the Dalai Lama: When asked what surprised him most, the Dalai Lama said: "Man, because he sacrifices his health in order to make money. Then he sacrifices money to recuperate his health. And then he is so anxious about the future that he does not enjoy the present; the result being that he does not live in the present or the future; he lives as if he is never going to die, and then he dies having never really lived."

So if more money is not the only answer to living a better life, what is the rest of the story?

That story is the one you choose to write for yourself – one that doesn't require a check or credit card payment. The path to the "good life" is under your control right now, no matter your income.

Tal Ben-Shahar, a Harvard University professor and author of *Happier*, says most of us can increase our happiness by engaging in life in these ways:

- Do what you enjoy. Get out your schedule and reserve time to do activities that are fun and fulfilling. Making time for yourself doesn't have to overburden your schedule, but it will increase your happiness.

- Express gratitude. Expressing gratitude takes your focus off of what you deem to be negative and puts it on the positive. Suddenly, you have a new mindset and a new appreciation of life.

- Set and work toward meaningful goals. Positive emotions arise when we work toward meaningful goals, and as we continue to learn, take on new challenges, and live with purpose. This type of happiness is called eudaimonic well-being, which is more robust and satisfying than hedonic happiness.

17

- Use your strengths. From the field of positive psychology, there is ample evidence that people who use their strengths are happier. Not sure what your strengths are? Check out www.strengthsfinder.com or the book *Strengths Finder 2.0*.

- Simplify your life. These days it is easy to find yourself overwhelmed by possessions, commitments, and obligations. If you are, it's time to stop. Make a list of the changes you need to make, then take action.

Your income is just one small part of your happiness formula. The rest is up to you. Go for it.

7

THE UNEXPECTED BENEFITS OF CUTTING BACK

Right now, you have many reasons to worry about money. But all is not doom and gloom; even these clouds can have a silver lining.

Let's look at five unexpected benefits cutting back.

Time with family and friends

Cutting back on the "go-go lifestyle" that characterized over commitment and over spending has allowed many families to spend less money and spend more time together.

The unexpected benefit: Socially connected people live longer, respond better to stress, have stronger immune systems and fare better when fighting many illnesses than those who are not as socially connected, according to medical researchers.

Preparing your own meals

Cutting back on going out to eat is a common strategy for saving money, whether it's staying in for dinner or brown-bagging your lunch.

19

By my calculation, you can save about $1,200 per year by bringing your lunch four times per week and eating out just once.

The unexpected benefit: Preparing meals at home can be healthier. Many popular restaurant meals have more than 2,000 calories. So reducing the number of times, you splurge will help your pocketbook and your waistline.

A simplified life

Selling nonessential possessions can be a useful and quick way to raise money when times are tight.

The unexpected benefit: Having less stuff reduces your stress levels. As Leo Babauta, creator of www.ZenHabits.net, says, disorganization stresses us out. The more stuff you are responsible for, the more difficult it is to be organized and the more stress you experience.

Volunteering

Being let go from a job can be one of the scariest and most stressful events in life. If you lose your job, volunteering can be an effective way to learn new skills, network, and get out of the house.

The unexpected benefit: Recent layoffs and job losses have led to a significant increase in volunteerism. The Corporation for National and Community Service reported nearly 27 percent of U.S. adults volunteered in 2009.

Working part-time

Many people who were expecting to retire fully have had to cut back on their leisure time and go back to work to protect their retirement savings. Others who were expecting to work full-time for a few more years have been unable to find full-time work. Many of them have sought part-time employment.

The unexpected benefit: Working part-time can provide important financial and emotional rewards. By working part-time, you may be able to use your experience to help a small company that is unable to hire a full-time employee as it gets started. And as a friend of mine recently said: "Many people just don't do retirement very well."

Yes, prolonged economic crisis can be difficult, and it may be some time before you dig out of your financial hole. But if we can make the best of these difficult circumstances, we may find an unexpected silver lining in the clouds.

8

CURB CONSUMPTION, REDUCE CLUTTER, FEEL AT PEACE

What would it be like if there were no economic barriers to consuming as much as we wanted?

Well, many of us are essentially living like that already. Consider this:

- If 100 kids represented all the children in the world and there were 100 toys for them, the three American kids would own 40.
- The average weight of the contents of an American home is 8,000 pounds – about the same as 40 pigs ready for market or one full-grown hippo.
- There are 48,500 storage facilities in the U.S., more than all the McDonald's, Burger Kings, Wendy's, and Starbucks combined.

When did our overconsumption start?

About 30 years ago, we began spending nearly half of our incomes on non-necessities. In the mid-1980s, consumer goods declined in price, credit card usage increased, and big-box stores and discount retailers established themselves. Today, for many Americans, this illusion of luxury feeds easy and prolific consumption.

A century ago, consumer choices were limited. I'm glad that's not true today; however, one-click shopping has virtually eliminated our ability to second-guess our impulses to buy.

We are failing to ask critical questions: Do I need this? Will I actually use it? How long will it last? Could I borrow it? Could I do without it? Where will I put it?

When my sister and I cleaned out our parents' home when they moved to a nursing home, I knew we needed a dumpster. The dumpster service was out of the 6-cubic-yard size like you might find in an alley behind a business, so I got a 30-cubic-yard dumpster, which you might see at a construction site.

We filled it – to the top. We also had a garage sale and gave a bunch of things to charity.

If stuff led to happiness, we would be the happiest society in the history of the world. The opposite seems to be true. A home with too much stuff can lead to anxiety.

UCLA anthropologist Elinor Ochs, who studies hyper acquisition, says our "stuffocation" may be both a symptom and a cause of this anxiety. Cluttered rooms can provoke the release of the stress hormone cortisol. For many Americans, the antidote to stress is shopping, which leads to the release of dopamine and temporary euphoria. Hence, the consumption trap.

There is another way.

The Life-Changing Magic of Tidying Up by Marie Kondo helped my wife, Cheri, and I clear out hundreds of items of clutter and reduce our anxiety. This best-selling book encourages readers to create long-term serenity by getting rid of everything that does not spark joy.

If you want more serenity, consider less stuff.

9

HOW DO YOU FEEL ABOUT YOUR FINANCES?

When I was deeply in debt, the last thing I wanted to do was acknowledge my feelings about my finances. By ignoring those feelings, I could ignore the reality of my situation.

Emotions can be intimately tied to how we manage our money – or how we fail to manage it. How do you feel about your finances? Right now, take a minute to reflect on those feelings. Then, complete this sentence: I feel _____ about my finances.

You may be feeling angry, sad, or afraid, or you may be feeling happy, proud, or content. Maybe you're ambivalent. If you have negative feelings about your money management, it's time to examine why. And, in my experience, you don't necessarily have to be in debt to be feeling miserable about your money.

Emotional discontent over your finances is likely to indicate that your earning, spending, and saving choices are not getting you what you truly value. Sure, you may be getting some benefit from those choices, but it's likely that you are trading long-term, deep satisfaction for momentary, fleeting pleasure.

I arrived at the dead end of my finance path by following someone else's vision and measure of happiness. I was traveling the road of consumerism: the belief that personal happiness can be obtained through buying products and services – a philosophy epitomized by phrases such as "he who dies with the most toys wins," "shop till you drop" and "retail therapy."

One of the early signs of trouble for me came when I was preparing to go on a weeklong business trip. It was easier for me to buy all new shirts, socks, and underclothing than to do laundry. All the while, I lamented that if the house cleaner would do the laundry too, everything would be perfect. Later, thinking about this made me angry and sad that I had let my life and finances get so out of control.

Frustration, anger, or despair about your finances signal the need for change, and a dream can give you something to strive for. In my last column, I discussed the importance of having a dream. A dream can be a guiding light in building a path to financial stability and emotional peace.

If you feel like a change is in order, you may be wondering where to begin. Start by asking yourself where you are today and where you want to be in the future.

Assess your current situation by determining:

- Your household's monthly take-home income.
- Everything you spend money on – this will become your budget.
- How much debt you have, excluding your mortgage.
- If you have enough savings for a $1,000 emergency fund or, better yet, a three- to a six-month emergency fund.

Decide where you want to go by determining:

- The dream that will motivate you.
- How much money you will need to be financially independent.

Once you know where you are on your personal-finance path, you can begin creating a plan to manage your money and begin identifying the roadblocks that may keep you from your goal.

Personal-finance roadblocks will be the next topic.

10

ELIMINATE YOUR FINANCE ROADBLOCKS

Succeeding in any endeavor depends on knowing where you are and where you want to go. And when it comes to aspects of your life like personal finance, wellness or physical fitness, you also must be aware of the roadblocks standing between you and your goals.

Goals that require daily discipline can be sabotaged by misguided behaviors and beliefs – or what I call roadblocks. Each of us creates a personal-finance reality through the choices we make, and these choices can include the roadblocks we build. Fortunately, because we put up these obstacles to success, we also can take them down.

Some common personal-finance roadblocks are:

- Not knowing how much money your household earns and/or spends each month.
- Using credit cards instead of cash.
- Having debt instead of saving for future purchases.
- Believing that you are stuck and can't change your situation.
- Keeping separate finances from your partner.

Now, it's time to identify your roadblocks. What's keeping you from achieving your dreams? What behaviors or beliefs do you need to change? What new habits do you need to cultivate?

Make a list and be honest with yourself – honesty is important and, yes, it may be difficult, too. These are the financial choices that are getting between you and your dreams.

Not having a budget and not saving for future purchases were my two biggest roadblocks. For me, not planning and not saving resulted in credit-card debt. Without a realistic, written budget to guide me, I was unaware of my spending habits and patterns.

Knowing your roadblocks is the critical first step to overcoming them. Most of the time, the behavior needed to break down your roadblocks will be obvious. But what may not be obvious is what those obstacles are keeping you from achieving.

Once you have made your list, I encourage you to develop a short and clear statement about your roadblocks and what they cost you. For example, my statement is: Debt and unconscious spending steal my dreams. For a couple that keeps their finances separated the roadblock statement could be: TEAM – Together Each Achieves More.

Once you have identified your barriers to success, it's time to create an action plan. What can you do in the next 30 days to begin overcoming each of your roadblocks? Be specific, be realistic, and be committed. Set goals you can achieve.

Don't worry; you don't have to overcome your roadblocks and be done with them forever in just a month. These hurdles will likely be with you for a long time. They will take work to defeat once and for all. The difference is that now you can see them, and now you can begin to replace them with more productive behaviors and beliefs.

If you take the steps necessary to overcome your personal-finance roadblocks, I assure you that you'll begin to feel better about your financial situation and you'll see a move a step – or several steps – closer to achieving your dreams.

11

THE PSYCHOLOGY OF MONEY: TAKE CONTROL OF YOUR SHADOWS

Money touches every aspect of our lives and occupies our thoughts daily.

When our thoughts about money turn negative, I call them "money shadows." Psychologist Carl Jung popularized the term "shadow," which means a belief about yourself that you hide, repress, or deny. Very often, these beliefs are negative judgments.

So our negative thoughts about money aren't really about money at all – they are reflections of the negative beliefs we have about ourselves. The sources of these shadows are the emotional wounds we experienced as children. Yes, each of us has experienced events that caused us to create negative beliefs about ourselves.

Some common shadows are: "I'm not worthy of love or attention," "I don't matter," "I don't deserve success" and, one of my shadows, "I'm stupid."

Money is a powerful trigger for shadows because of the power it has in our culture. For most people, money has come to mean more than its dictionary definition of something generally accepted as a medium of exchange, a measure of value or a means of payment.

In our culture, money and the things money can buy have become equated with security, power, beauty, social acceptance, sex appeal, and success. It's easy for our financial challenges and missteps to trigger shadows.

For example, if someone has the shadow of not being worthy of love or attention and equates money with social acceptance, any negative financial change may cause that person to feel excluded or unworthy. Or, a person who doubts his ability to succeed and equates money with power may be paralyzed by fear when it comes to seeking a promotion or advocating for a raise.

Shadow beliefs can create a cycle of stress and unhappiness: When they block you from getting what you value because you feel inherently unworthy, you are unlikely to attain what you want, and you will feel even more unworthy.

But there is a way out of the cycle, and these steps can help:

- Listen to those gremlins of negative self-talk. Don't believe them, but become familiar with what they say. They will begin to reveal your shadows.

- Make time to talk with your partner or a close friend, and share your shadows. They seem to have less of a hold on us when we shine some light them.

- Make a list of what money – and the things it can buy – means to you. Be honest with yourself; you don't have to show the list to anyone.

- Make a list of what's most important to you in your life.

- Think about your financial behavior and see if your actions are being driven by your shadows or what's most important in your life.

- Take action to align your behavior with what's most important to you.

Becoming conscious of your underlying beliefs about yourself and money will make you a better consumer and a better manager of your money. And, more importantly, consciousness will decrease your stress and increase your happiness.

12

YOU CAN STOP LIVING PAYCHECK TO PAYCHECK

An article in *The Atlantic* and $700 in car maintenance got me to thinking about unexpected expenses.

The article, *The Secret Shame of Middle-Class Americans*, reveals how nearly half of us don't have enough savings to cover an unexpected $400 expense. Many of us are living on the financial edge, hoping and praying no one sees behind the mask that says, "I'm fine," "I can handle it," "I'm doing OK."

If you are struggling and feeling shame, there are two things you can do to address your situation and change your future. You can use this approach for any personal challenge, not just financial issues.

First, you must break the shame cycle. Brene Brown, shame and vulnerability researcher, and author says that shame needs three things to grow: silence, secrecy, and judgment. To break the cycle, you must talk about it with someone you trust to end the silence and bring it out of the shadows.

Second, you must confront the problem. For me, that means getting it down on paper so I can see it, and all of its parts. Only then can I take action.

If you're struggling with your finances, talk to a trusted friend, release yourself from that silent burden and create a plan of action to take control of your earning, spending, and saving.

Here are 15 ways you can improve your financial health so you can cover the next unexpected expense.

1. Live on a budget – it's like getting a 30 percent raise!

2. Get a second job or work overtime. This is not a long-term solution, but there's nothing like working more to earn more money.

3. Sell unwanted items on eBay or Craigslist. This is an easy way to raise cash.

4. Stop going out to lunch. In a single month, you can save $200.

5. Bring your coffee or tea to work. Stop spending $2 to $5 a day on a drink you can make at home.

6. Stop drinking soda and energy drinks — another simple way to save hundreds of dollars a year.

7. Quit smoking. A pack-a-day smoker will save about $1,450 a year.

8. Eat dinner at home. Two fewer meals out a month will save about $420 annually.

9. Stop buying junk food. Just $10 less each week is a savings of $520 a year.

10. Drop cable/satellite TV and save hundreds.

11. Pay with cash. Studies show that people spend 12 to 30 percent more when they use a credit card.

12. Get rid of that storage unit (and sell what you don't need/want). Stop renting a house for your extra stuff.

13. Make sure you have the right insurance, which can also save you hundreds of dollars a year.

14. Cancel your landline. If the home phone is ringing, it must be a telemarketer, right?

15. With your newfound savings, build an emergency fund of $1,000.

These simple measures to save and earn more can prepare you for life's financial curveballs.

13

HOW TO END FINANCIAL CHAOS AND WORRY

"I'm worried about money," a friend confessed to me the other day.

I assured her that she's not alone, and neither are you if you're worried about money. A recent survey by Varo revealed that 85 percent of us worry about money. Thirty percent worry constantly!

The survey illuminated that:

- 66 percent of American adults do not have a three-month emergency fund.
- 46 percent don't have any savings set aside for unexpected expenses.
- And for 33 percent, financial chaos would ensue if they lost a job, were injured or their car broke down.

Worry and stress are a natural reaction to these facts, but stress doesn't have to be part of your financial reality.

Here are the actions I recommended to my friend:

1. Accumulate $500 as soon as possible by selling some gear or household items.

2. Make a list of all of your debts from smallest to largest.

3. Create a realistic budget that includes:

    a. Basic necessities: housing, groceries, utilities, and gas.

    b. Obligations: credit card payments and other debts.

    c. Less-than-monthly expenditures, such as car repairs.

    d. Nice-to-have expenses, such as entertainment, coffee and restaurants.

4. Follow your budget and update it each month. It will take a few months to get the kinks worked out.

5. Stop using all credit cards.

6. Use cash for all discretionary spending.

7. Get a second job or start a side hustle to earn an extra $1,000 per month.

8. Negotiate for a raise.

9. Get a roommate or rent extra space in your home through Airbnb.

10. Celebrate small wins and accomplishments.

11. Build a small $1,000 emergency fund by selling more stuff and saving monthly.

12. After the $1,000 is safely in the bank for emergencies, use the original $500 to cover unexpected expenses or what I call less-than-monthly expenses.

13. Keep adding monthly to your savings for less-than-monthly expenses.

14. Squeeze your budget and use the money to pay off credit cards and other on-mortgage debts, starting with the smallest on the list.

15. When all non-mortgage debts are paid off, grow the $1,000 emergency fund to a three-month emergency fund.

16. Have proper levels of insurance:

    e. Auto

    f. Renters/homeowners

    g. Short- and long-term disability

    h. Life

17. Build your professional skills and network before you need to find a new job.

These action steps might seem overwhelming. Take one step at a time, and work on taking control of your financial life a little each week.

While the entire process of paying off all of your debt and saving an emergency fund equal to three months of living expenses is likely to take 12 to 36 months, the stress and worry will vanish quickly.

Then you will be among the 15 percent of the people who don't worry about money.

14

TIME FOR A FINANCIAL CHECK-UP

How do you feel about your financial health? Are you anxious and insecure, secure and happy, or somewhere in between?

The symptoms of financial stress can be many. The American Institute of Certified Public Accountants says they include:

- A growing waistline, as junk food becomes a coping strategy.
- Diminished friendships, as people become more irritable and find less time for friendships.
- Interrupted sleep, as worries invade the nighttime hours.

Annual checkups are recommended to keep us in good health and to detect problems early. I recommend an annual financial checkup for the same reasons. An assessment of your finances can help you avoid potential problems and remedy existing ailments while they are small enough to manage easily.

This week, we'll start with a personal-finance checkup. Next week, we'll look at prescriptions for a secure financial future.

Answer "yes" or "no" to these questions:

1. Do you have a written budget that you revise regularly and follow each month?

2. Does your budget include accumulating money for purchases made on a less-than-monthly basis, such as insurance or tires?

3. Do you have medical insurance?

4. Do you have short-term disability insurance?

5. Do you have long-term disability insurance?

6. Do you have life insurance?

7. Do you have an emergency fund equal to at least three months of living expenses?

8. Are you spending less than 35 percent of your take-home pay on housing (rent, mortgage, property taxes, homeowners' association fees)?

9. Do you pay for purchases with only cash or debit cards?

10. Are you investing 15 percent of your take-home pay for the purpose of achieving financial independence?

11. Are you saving for your children's college fund at a rate that will allow them to attend a four-year institution without using student loans?

12. Are you paying on your mortgage at a rate that will allow you to pay it off in 15 years?

13. Do you work at your job because it's your passion?

14. Has it been more than three months since you worried about money?

15. Do you have a dream toward which you are moving deliberately? If you have a partner, is it a shared dream?

Give yourself one point for each "yes" and see how you rank.

- 0-4 points: Financial stress level is very high. It's time to take control of spending and money management.
- 5-9 points: Financial stress level is moderate to high. With a series of changes, financial security can be yours.
- 10-12 points: Financial stress level is moderate to low. Just a few changes will give you financial security.
- 13-15 points: Financial stress is low. Congratulations, you have true financial security.

Many factors can contribute to a lower score than you would like. This assessment is a starting point for understanding your behavior and choices. By consciously considering your financial situation, you can make the right changes.

Next, we'll look at the prescription for less stress and more happiness.

15

A Prescription For Your Financial Wellness

Financial health, just like personal health, depends on consistently making good choices. There's no magic pill to lose 50 pounds or to erase all of your debts.

Financial security is a deliberate choice, and being realistic about your current situation is the beginning of being able to choose a path toward security and happiness.

Chapter 9 was about making choices that lead to financial security. If you missed it, go back and take the financial assessment based on 15 questions. The more you answered "yes," the healthier your finances.

Budgeting

- Do you have a written budget that guides your spending and is revised regularly?
- Does your budget include accumulating money for purchases made on a less-than-monthly basis?

Having a budget and saving for future purchases helps eliminate "emergencies" and allows you to take day-to-day control of your spending. For example, enjoying the holidays is a lot easier when you're accumulating money in advance.

Insurance

- Do you have medical insurance, short-term disability insurance, long-term disability insurance, and life insurance?

Insurance helps you replace what you can't afford to replace. This includes your income, through short- and long-term disability coverage. Your income is your greatest wealth-building tool.

An emergency fund

- Do you have an emergency fund equal to at least three months of living expenses?

The last thing you need in an emergency is debt. An emergency fund can see you through the unexpected. As little as $1,000 is a good start. Three to six months of living expenses is ideal.

Overspending: Don't

- Are you spending less than 35 percent of your take-home pay on housing?
- Do you pay for purchases only with cash or a debit card?

Overspending limits your ability to harness your income as a wealth-building tool. Credit cards can lead to overspending by 10 percent to 40 percent.

The future: Have a plan

- Are you investing 15 percent of your take-home pay for the purpose of achieving financial independence?
- Are you saving for your children's college fund at a rate that will allow them to attend a four-year institution without using student loans?
- Are you paying on your mortgage at a rate that will allow you to pay it off in 15 years?

Planning for your future means implementing systems. Automatic savings and investing plans and 15-year mortgages create results without requiring monthly action.

Passion and dreams

- Do you work at your job because it's your passion?
- Has it been more than three months since you worried about money?
- Do you have a dream toward which you are moving deliberately? If you have a partner, is it a shared dream?

Dreams and a passion for work are antidotes to consumerism. Passionately pursuing your dream keeps you focused on what's most important and prevents you from foolishly shopping for satisfaction.

The more you can say "yes" to these questions over time, the more you will reduce your financial stress and increase your financial security.

16

ENRICH YOURSELF WITH AN ATTITUDE OF CELEBRATION, GRATITUDE

During the last two columns, I've asked you to undergo a financial check-up and write a prescription for improving your financial health. If you're like me, these exercises can turn up mistakes I've made and show me what I should be doing differently.

Those mistakes can be upsetting and discouraging, but beating ourselves up about poor choices or difficult circumstances won't help us create the lives we want. Turning our attention toward the positive aspects of our lives, no matter what challenges we may face at the moment will serve us well.

"Gratitude enriches human life. It elevates, energizes, inspires, and transforms. People are moved, opened and humbled through expressions of gratitude," says Robert Emmons, University of California, Davis, professor, and author of *Thanks! How the New Science of Gratitude Can Make You Happier*. "Without gratitude, life can be lonely, depressing, and impoverished."

I would like you to pause, reflect, and express gratitude for what is working in your life. The positive psychology movement shows that people who consistently express gratitude are:

- more positive
- more likely to improve their health
- better able to deal with adversity
- more connected to other people

And the result is that they are happier.

Sometimes, we are so focused on our goals that we fail to reflect on our accomplishments. This can leave us in a constant state of dissatisfaction. Do you have a habit of doing this? If so, it's time to develop an attitude of celebration and gratitude.

Gratitude

Begin practicing gratitude by making a list. Select a new notebook or journal for this project – a few pieces of paper can work just as well.

I'm grateful for Moleskine notebooks. The way they feel in my hands reminds me that I live in a world where artists create joy through sensory experience.

Your journal entries will be simple, but they can have a profound impact. Each day – set aside a regular time in the morning or evening – list what makes you feel grateful. You may need to start small: a walk in the sun or a warm cup of coffee, for example. From there, continue your list. Add to it until you can't think of anything else. Then, leave a space for one more.

Celebration

Each time you reach a milestone on your way to a goal, mark it with a small celebration.

Recently, a friend told me that he and his wife have pizza every night they reach a milestone. They take time to recognize their progress, and a small splurge makes them feel good. These rituals of celebration can serve as motivation and reward. They are significant reminders of our progress.

For me, this quote from Oprah Winfrey sums up the value and importance of gratitude: "Be thankful for what you have; you'll end up having more. If you concentrate on what you don't have, you will never, ever have enough."

17

DO IT YOURSELF: BREAK THE HABIT OF OVERSPENDING

Do you have the nagging feeling that you may be overspending when you buy groceries or go out to eat? After all, it's so easy to add extras to your cart or head to your favorite restaurant when the cupboard is empty – and along the way bust your budget.

Recently at a part, a friend told me: "I've got the best budget in the world – I just don't follow it."

When he and his wife are tired, they succumb to the temptation to eat out even if they are exceeding their monthly limit for restaurant dinners. And to make the potential for overspending even greater, they based their eating out on a number of nights, not a dollar amount.

Temptation and undisciplined spending can make the best budget irrelevant. Overspending can be so easy. But sticking to your budget can be easy, too.

The best way I've found to interrupt a pattern of overspending and adhere to my budget is the cash envelope system. Envelopes give you a visual reminder of your commitment and a place to hold the actual money available to you. There's no guessing game, no rationalizing, no pretending.

You can buy a fancy cash envelope system, subscribe to an online system such as Mvelopes or build your own. I recommend that you do it yourself.

Building your system is not difficult and costs almost nothing. To get started, you will need five to seven envelopes. They can be new or used, and they can be any size that works for you.

Then decide what spending you will pay in cash from your envelopes. Customize your system. What works for you does not need to work for anyone else.

I recommend these categories:

- Groceries
- Restaurants
- Entertainment
- Spontaneous spending
- Gasoline
- Miscellaneous

You also might consider coffee, lunch, clothing, and any other spontaneously purchased items. Clearly label the envelopes on the front and back because they serve as visual reminders of your commitment to living by your budget.

Hint: You may need to create a set of envelopes for yourself and your partner, especially for categories such as restaurants, spending, and gasoline.

Now it's time to decide how much you will spend each month in each category.

I recommend you take money out of each paycheck to fill your envelopes. For example, if you budgeted $300 a month for groceries and you get paid twice a month, take $150 from each paycheck.

When you get your cash, don't forget to get the right quantity of bills so you can divide your money properly. For example, you can't get all $20 bills if you budget $150 for your grocery envelope.

With your envelopes labeled and filled, you are ready to interrupt that pattern of overspending. Sure, you can still decide to go out to dinner despite having an empty restaurant envelope. But this choice is likely to be more deliberate and conscious rather than an impulsive decision that leaves you with the nagging feeling you aren't in control of your money.

18

STOP IT! YOU'RE SPENDING TOO MUCH. NO, YOU ARE

"Please, will you tell him (or her) to stop spending so much money?"

I frequently receive this question from people who want my advice about their partner's spending habits.

Invariably, I say, "No," because what they are asking me is to tell their partner to spend money in accordance with their desires.

Psychologist David Myers makes an illuminating observation: "The only chance of satisfaction we can imagine is getting more of what we have now. But what we have now makes everybody dissatisfied. So what will more of it do – make us more satisfied or dissatisfied?"

What can a couple do when they get stuck in a recurring conflict about spending? The solution lies in creating a shared sense of purpose – and being willing to compromise.

Beginning a conversation about money, compromise, and purpose can be difficult. Approach this talk with thought and planning.

For starters, mention how you are feeling about your finances and suggest that the two of you talk at a quiet, relaxed time. Slowly moving into the conversation puts the topic out in the open and can prevent your partner from feeling ambushed.

Schedule a date. I suggest a weekend walk or coffee. Walking can get you out in nature and may open you to possibilities beyond material satisfaction. Your talk should include both of your hopes and dreams so you can begin to form a shared vision for the future.

Take care not to blame your partner. Blame can be a way for us to vent our pain and disappointment – you may be disappointed with your partner's financial choices because they have gotten in the way of your dreams. Instead of blaming, try to express how you feel. Being willing to take ownership of your feelings may help your partner open up and share, too.

More often than we realize, dissatisfaction in one or more areas of our life begins to creep into our finances. Is this happening to either of you?

If you can both acknowledge a desire for change, it's time to look to the future. My preference is to approach this type of change holistically. Consider a variety of goals: financial, physical, mental, family, spiritual, lifestyle, and relationship.

Make your goals concrete by getting a journal to write them down. Each of you should take a few hours alone in a quiet place to ask yourself what has been going well in these areas, what needs improvement, and how do you want to feel? Finally, what do you want to accomplish in the next 12 to 18 months?

Then come back together to talk about what you've written. See how close or how far apart your perspectives are in each area.

In places where you are far apart, take time to share your ideas and listen carefully to one another, with the intent of truly understanding what your partner is saying and feeling. Use this as an opportunity to develop mutually beneficial goals and support one another.

Shared goals or dreams can be the stars that guide your relationship and guide you away from conflicts about money.

19

YOU VS. THE GROCERY STORE

Your grocery store and the brands it sells are out to shape your behavior to pull every dollar out of your pocket possible.

Yes, much of what retail marketers do increases the pleasure of our shopping experience, a good thing. But because we make frequent trips to the supermarket, overspending can cost you thousands of dollars a year. Not good.

Let the battle begin!

Here are some of the ways grocery-store marketers attempt to influence your buying behavior.

1. Flowers, fruit, and bakery items in the front of the store offer bright colors and welcoming sights that make us feel like a guest, lower our guard, and spend more.

2. The color of products and signs influence perception and buying. As many as 90 percent of us decide on a product in 90 seconds or less just based on color.

3. The smell of fresh bread and prepared foods trigger hunger at prime shopping times, such as after work.

4. Eating samples engages our taste, hunger, and reciprocity. When given something, we are more likely to return the favor by making a purchase.

5. Music with a slower tempo can cause shoppers to unconsciously linger to buy more.

6. "Eye level is buying level." More expensive products are at adult eye level, while store brands are placed higher or lower.

7. Kids' cereal is on the bottom shelf – kids' eye level.

8. Dairy and eggs are placed at the back of the store to make us run the grocery-store gauntlet when all we need is a gallon of milk.

9. Impulse items are placed by the register. Willpower is like a muscle. After saying "no" to all of those other treats, we often say "yes" when we check out.

10. Shopping carts. Oversize carts look empty when they're not, and small carts with wheels allow us to shop more without the burden of a heavy basket.

11. Coupons. They may lead us to buy items we don't need or to ignore a sale on a comparable product that would be less expensive.

12. 10 for $10 sales. Did you really need ten cans of black beans?

13. Large package sizes or bulk may not be the bargain you think.

14. Signs advertising sales may draw you in to buy a more expensive brand.

15. Prices that end in .99 play on the left-digit effect, where our brains focus on the first number.

Here's how you can fight back:

- Be aware that people are working on getting you to spend more.
- Use a budget.
- Plan your meals for the week.
- Make a grocery list.
- Compare prices by the ounce.
- Pay with cash.
- Don't shop when hungry.

Using these seven strategies can help you overcome most of the retail marketers' tricks.

Good luck!

20

$100 GROCERY BUDGET - SAVE UP TO $8000

$100. That's our food budget each week for our family of three; including a teenage boy. And we each take our lunch to school/work nearly every day. By my calculations, we're saving between $1,800 and $8,000 per year compared to many families our size.

We eat very well. On that $100 a week we're eating delicious, nutritious, well-rounded meals with enough leftover for lunches.

How I Calculated Our Savings

You can use the USDA cost of food at home chart, http://bit.ly/CostofFoodAtHomeChart, to see how you compare to other families. There are four spending levels: Thrifty, Low-cost, Moderate-cost, and Liberal, that account for age, gender, and family size.

For the thrifty plan, an average family of three with a teenage boy spends $135.77 each week. At $100 per week, we save more than

$1800 each year compared to the thriftiest families and an astronomical $8000 more than the liberal shoppers.

Sometimes we go over our $100 budget, usually because of laundry detergent, toiletries, and the like, so our real spending may be a little closer to the Thrifty average, but nowhere near the Liberal plan.

What food plan are you on?

Determine how much you spent last month at the grocery store. Then use the cost of food chart above to compare your spending to the four different grocery store spending levels.

The Average American

The Bureau of Labor Statistics data gives us some insight into the average US spending on groceries in an article called How the Average US Consumer Spends Their Paycheck, http://bit.ly/PaycheckDWesley, by Daniel Wesley.

Spending on food comes in third behind transportation and housing with $6,602 spent on food: $3,977 on food eaten at home and $2,625 on meals and snacks away from home.

Based on the average income before taxes of $63,784 cited, grocery spending is 6.2% of the average household's earnings. That means a family who spends liberally on groceries, $13,328.12, would have an expected annual income of nearly $215,000.

You can use the same calculation to check your grocery spending. Multiply your weekly grocery spending by 52 weeks to get your annual spending. Then divide by .062 to find the corresponding expected income.

- Do you spend more or less than $100/week?
- How would you classify your grocery budget: Thrifty, Low-Cost, Moderate, or Liberal?
- What percentage of your income are you spending on groceries?
- Are you overspending on groceries?

Next, I'll show you how we manage to keep our grocery budget to just $100 a month.

21

THE SECRET TO $100 GROCERY BUDGET REVEALED

My family of three eats delicious, healthy meals on a grocery budget of $100 a week, with enough leftovers for lunch. How do we do it? The secret is quite simple, and you can do it, too.

We use this four-step process for planning and spending: review the week; plan the menu; complete the grocery list, and shop using a cash envelope.

Review the week

I begin by considering what's going on in the evenings during the upcoming week and pick meals that fit the time we have for cooking.

On a piece of paper, I list the days of the week and what's going on each evening. It looks something like this:

- Saturday: Out with friends.
- Sunday: Evening at home.
- Monday: Matt, ManKind Project board meeting.

- Tuesday: Work out at the gym as a family.
- Wednesday: Matt, MKP group.
- Thursday: Our son, Malcolm, goes to fencing.
- Friday: Evening at home.

Plan the menu

With our schedule for the week set, I grab some of my favorite cookbooks and start meal planning.

This week, I picked:

- Road to Morocco Lamb with Pine Nut Couscous for Sunday and Wednesday.
- Carrot Muffins on a Grid on Monday. Breakfast for dinner is a simple meal, and we'll have waffles for the rest of the week.
- Southwestern Corn and Potato Soup and sandwiches for a quick and easy meal on Tuesday night after our trip to the gym.
- Pumpkin Polenta with Chorizo and Black Beans on Thursday when I'll have more time to cook.

Grocery list

Once I've picked out the recipes, I get our pre-printed grocery list off the refrigerator door. We keep it there so that we can quickly highlight items when we run out during the week.

With highlighter in hand, I review each recipe and highlight the ingredients we need or write them on the list if they are ingredients we don't use frequently enough to include on the pre-printed list. After making sure I have everything I need for meals, I turn my attention to other basics that we'll need for the week, including lunches.

You can get a copy of our pre-printed grocery list at http://bit.ly/Pre-PrintedGroceryList.

Grocery shopping

Now, it's off to the store with our cash envelope. Sticking to $100 might seem hard. After all, it's so easy to drop extras into your cart and bust your budget.

We follow these four guidelines to avoid overspending:

- Take just $100 cash with you.
- Unload the most needed items from your cart first.
- Stick to your list.
- Avoid stocking up. Buy only as much as you need.

Give this method a try for a month and see how much money you save.

22

MAKE A CHOICE TO MAKE LASTING CHANGE

If you have resolved to take control of your finances. I want to help you get started today. This is the first column in a four-part series, chapter 22 – 25, designed to give you the tools to achieve financial well-being.

Why start now? Because change can be difficult. Making a real change, especially when it comes to your finances, takes time, effort, and focus. You need to learn and practice new patterns of behavior.

Changing behavior can be so hard because our minds are controlled by two different systems: the emotional and the rational. The rational side wants to retire wealthy and secure, and the emotional side wants to go out to dinner – tonight!

In *The Happiness Hypothesis*, Jonathan Haidt compares these two aspects of our minds to an elephant (emotional) and a rider (rational). Picture a rider atop an elephant. The tiny rider can exert control over the elephant only occasionally and only for a short time. Like the elephant, our emotions can be powerful, sometimes uncontrollable, forces.

Many of the changes we aspire to involve giving up instant gratification (emotional desire) and pursuing long-term goals (rational desire). To achieve those goals, we need to work with the strengths and weaknesses of both the emotional and rational aspects of ourselves. When they work in harmony, rather than in opposition, we can achieve the change we seek.

Authors Dan and Chip Heath, in their book *Switch*, describe how we can direct the rider, motivate the elephant, and shape a path. This chapter we'll give the rider direction. In chapter 23, we'll focus on motivation; in chapter 24, we'll shape the path, and in chapter 25, we'll put it all together.

So today, let's set a direction by identifying one dream. I prefer vacations or adventures because they are achievable and inspiring. By the end of November, I want you, and your partner if you have one, to have picked a dream and created a dream board.

A dream board provides a goal to focus your actions. It's the incentive to change. Using pictures is effective because they tap into the emotional side of our minds and can be strong motivators.

Creating a dream board is a powerful and fun process. Here's how:

1. Get a large piece of paper or poster board.

2. Gather magazines with images of your dream vacation destination or adventure.

3. Find your perfect picture and glue it in the center of your paper.

4. Glue supporting pictures around the central image.

5. Hang your dream board, where you can see it every day.

With your destination in sight, the journey can begin. Next chapter: Finding the motivation to make change stick.

23

TURN YOUR DREAMS INTO REALITY

"Vision without action is merely a dream.
Action without vision just passes the time.
Vision with action can change the world."
– Joel A. Barker, author, and futurist

Last chapter, I asked you to think about a dream vacation or adventure. I hope you brought your trip to life on the dream board to envision your goal fully.

Today, we are going to take action to turn your vision into reality.

- Step 1: See your goal. Go back to your dream board, search for your destination online, or if the idea came from a magazine, read the article again. Immerse yourself in thoughts of being at your destination.

- Step 2: Feel what it will be like. Take a few minutes to make an itinerary and outline the specific activities you will be doing. Then, describe your feelings. Are you calm, relaxed, exhilarated?

- Step 3: Action. Create a simple budget. A budget is a tool that will turn your desires into reality.

Think about what you will want and need for your trip. Research your options and be realistic. Remember, you can make this trip as simple or as deluxe as you choose.

Now, begin to sort out the details. The budget categories you'll want to use are transportation, lodging, meals, activities, spending money, and miscellaneous.

Using your research, do your best to estimate the costs accurately. Total the amounts you budgeted for each category. The total is what you need to save to make your trip a reality.

If the total seems too high, review each item in your budget to see how you can scale back. Less expensive lodging? Drive instead of fly? A self-guided tour instead of a guided trip? Be creative.

Your next decision is when to go. The timing is important because you'll need time to build up your savings. The goal is to pay for your trip before you go.

Divide the total amount you budgeted for the trip by the number of months until you want to go. Now you know the amount you'll need to set aside each month. If this goal seems too big, decide if you're willing to wait longer or if you would prefer to reduce your expenses.

To make this dream even more real, I suggest you open a special savings account specifically for this trip. Each month deposit your savings goal into the account.

You may even want to have the bank set up an automatic monthly withdrawal from your checking account into your savings account, so you're not tempted to skip a month.

Congratulations, you are now using the financially independent mindset! You created a vision for yourself; you researched it, planned a budget, evaluated your spending habits to accommodate your goal, and took action to begin saving for a future expense.

Next: Shape your path by tweaking your environment and building new habits.

24

ONE NEW, EASY MONEY HABIT

Now you have the opportunity to create a new habit that will both save you money and improve your health. You're going to tackle the largest discretionary spending category in your budget: groceries.

Discretionary spending encompasses all the purchases you can pay for immediately. This type of spending is different from an obligation. An obligation is an agreement or contract to pay off a debt or to make a repeat purchase over time. For example, an ATV would be a discretionary purchase until a loan is taken out to buy it, then the loan becomes a monthly obligation.

The larger your discretionary spending budget can be the better. Paying cash for purchases and gives you flexibility if your income changes. Paying cash can keep you out of debt. Once you charge a purchase to a credit card, it becomes an obligation, and statistics show that when you pay with a credit card, you're likely to spend 12 to 30 percent more than when you pay cash.

The cash-envelope system will help you keep your spending under control. This system uses a series of envelopes labeled with the intended use for the money and is designed to prevent overspending.

You can use cash envelopes for every discretionary purchase category in your budget. Today, the focus is on groceries. We're starting with groceries for several reasons:

1. It's easy to set a grocery budget.

2. The grocery store is a defined shopping destination.

3. Groceries are typically the single largest discretionary spending category.

4. Much of what we buy is neither necessary nor healthy, allowing you to reduce your overall spending.

Getting started with your grocery envelope is easy. Label it clearly, then set a spending goal – be frugal, but realistic. Put your monthly allowance in cash inside the envelope. At the beginning of the month, you will withdraw half of the total, and midway you will withdraw the second half.

When you shop, make a list before you leave. At the store, keep a rough total cost for what's in your cart and pay in cash from your envelope. When you check out, you may want to put the most important groceries on the counter first, so if you do go over budget, you can put back the least important items.

More conscious spending at the grocery store not only saves you money, but it can also have a direct effect on your health. A study in the *Journal of Consumer Research* reveals that shoppers who pay with cash are less likely to buy unhealthy foods (such as cookies, candy, and baked goods) than people who pay with credit or debit cards.

We'll bring the elements of dreams, budgets, and spending together to help you keep your resolution of getting your finances under control in the final chapter of this four-part series.

25

GOAL: CONTROL YOUR FINANCES

You can choose to make this the year you gain control of your finances and begin living your dreams.

This is the fourth in a series of columns about how to change your money habits for the new year. My three previous columns addressed identifying a dream, creating a budget, and managing discretionary spending. Today, I'll bring all of those ideas together.

Learning how to manage your money requires changing your behavior. Building new habits take time and effort. You need to balance the rational mind (saving) against the tug of emotional desire (spending).

So strong motivation is essential to meet the challenge of actually living by new habits. That motivation is a dream. I know you may be dreaming of escaping the burden of debt, but I am looking for deeper motivation: What would you do if you didn't have any debt?

This dream – whether it be traveling, vacation, or more time with family – must be powerful enough to change your day-to-day financial behavior.

Once you've identified your dream, it's time to create a budget to make that dream a reality. First, determine how much money your household brings in every month after taxes. To get an accurate figure, take a look at recent pay stubs.

I have three rules when creating a budget: it must be written down (in any form that works for you); before the start of the month, and your spending must follow your plan.

There are only four things that you can do with money: spend it, pay off debt, save it, and give it away.

Let's focus on spending first. When building a budget, divide your spending into obligatory and discretionary categories. Obligations are expenses like your mortgage or your credit card or car payments. Discretionary spending includes items like groceries, gas, and miscellaneous purchases.

Add up your monthly spending. Is it smaller or larger than your take-home pay? If expenses exceed income, reduce or eliminate some spending.

Now, your debt. Add up your total debt – those monthly obligations, not including your mortgage. Then divide by 12. The answer is the amount you would need to pay to be debt-free in 12 months. If that number seems too large, try 18 months.

Saving must be part of your budget, too. You should save each month for future expenses like insurance, car repairs, and holiday gifts. And remember that dream? Begin setting aside money so you can realize it. Yes, making savings a regular budget item may mean reducing your spending again. I didn't say this would be easy.

Lastly, giving. Don't forget to budget for your generosity. If paying off debt and saving are your top priorities, you can increase giving once you are debt-free.

With your dream in focus and a written budget in place, you are ready to build new money habits that will lead you toward financial independence and personal fulfillment.

26

CREATE TRUE FINANCIAL INDEPENDENCE

Every day I hear about people's dreams for financial independence, but every day, I also see people struggling on an endless treadmill. They work more to buy more to create more happiness. This is hardly surprising. Consumer marketing constantly tells us buying the "right product" will make our lives better.

A better life – including happiness and financial independence – is worth pursuing, and I believe the path to true financial independence also leads to happiness. The question is, how do we get there.

For me, true financial independence is more than being free of debt and money worries: it combines sound money management with quality of life.

I define financial independence as the ability to generate sufficient income from your assets to pay for basic necessities and lifestyle expenses. Yes, this is a big, long-term goal, and it is not nearly as urgent as creating a life that matches your deeply held values.

In "true financial independence." The "true" comes from adding quality of life to the equation. For example, I believe the quality of your life improves from slowing down and making your values more important than an impulse to buy something.

Again and again, I hear clients say they want to spend more time doing what's most important to them: deepening their relationships with family and friends; enjoying nature; volunteering to help others; and experiencing the world through travel. How is all of this possible?

Try this exercise: On a piece of paper or in your journal, create three columns. At the top of the first column, write "basic necessities," label the second column, "material things," and the third column, "time to." Now answer this question: "What do I need to be happy and peaceful?"

Take a deep breath and clear your mind. In each of the three columns, begin listing what is true for you. Don't worry about saying the right thing or trying to please anyone else. Your answers should be your own. Be as specific as you can.

For example, describe in detail what basic shelter means to you. For some people it might mean a yurt on 10 acres, for others it's a condo, and yet for others, it's a 5,000-square-foot home on 40 acres. For me, it's a two-bedroom, 863-square-foot condo in town.

When your list is complete, you will know what brings you happiness and peace. Now, take a look at your possessions and your calendar and compare your list with your life. Is there a difference between what you say will bring you happiness and peace and what you have purchased and how you spend your time?

If you see an inconsistency between the quality of life you have created and the quality of life you want, identify steps to bridge that gap – and take them.

Those steps should bring you closer to true financial independence. They will help you reflect your actual values in your budget and help you reduce your spending. Then you will have more money available to pay off debt, build an emergency fund, save for future purchases, or invest – all of which form the path to financial independence.

27

STEP BY STEP YOU CAN MASTER YOUR MONEY

When I picked up the 656-page tome, I was curious. During the bustle of Noel Night at Maria's Bookshop, Tony Robbins' new book grabbed my attention.

I was familiar with Robbins from his infomercials, self-help programs, and TED Talks, but I wasn't familiar with his financial advice. Could this weighty book deliver?

With *Money – Master the Game: 7 Simple Steps to Achieve Financial Freedom*, Robbins, who has advised U.S. presidents, CEOs, and top athletes, aims to help "regular" people successfully travel the path to economic independence.

In his first major book in 20 years, Robbins condenses wisdom gleaned from interviews with financial gurus, billionaires, and Nobel Prize winners. He was inspired to write this extensive guide after watching the documentary film "Inside Job," which examines Wall

Street's role in the 2008 economic meltdown. (For more about the film, visit http://bit.ly/MoneySavvy1-15.)

Does Robbins' big book work? The short answer: Yes, he delivers.

Don't be intimidated by this book's size. Robbins uses the unusual, but effective, style of bolding the most important text for readers who want to speed-read. His engaging, conversational voice makes dense topics come to life.

For me, *Money* takes off in Section 3, about 200 pages in when he begins examining the price of our dreams. Robbins asserts our dreams are the sum of five different aspirations.

- Financial security: You do not have to work to pay for the basics, including housing, utilities, food, transportation, or basic insurance.
- Financial vitality: The ability to meet your financial security and half of the cost of your small indulgences and luxuries without working.
- Financial independence: The interest from savings and return from your investments allow you to maintain your lifestyle without working.
- Financial freedom: You have financial independence and two to three significant luxuries.
- Absolute financial freedom: The freedom to live and give freely without worrying about money or working.

I believe this is a valuable approach to understanding our financial dreams. Reading these, I realized most people go directly to absolute financial freedom when considering their dreams. But dreaming of unlimited wealth leaves many people overwhelmed and unwilling to take action.

By breaking down our dreams into a series of steps, we can better assess how much money will be required to achieve each milestone, and we can accurately measure where we are on the path toward our ultimate goal.

I highly recommend reading *Money*. By using Robbins' strategies, I believe you will find that you are capable of achieving your financial dreams.

And remember what Mark Twain said: "The secret of getting ahead is getting started."

28

LET THIS SIMPLE RULE LEAD YOU TO FINANCIAL SUCCESS

Over the years, as I've helped people take control of their money and begin to live their dreams, I've discovered a simple, little-known rule that when applied, creates financial success.

It's easy to understand, but it can be difficult to use. If you do though, its power is transformative. I've seen people use it to pay off overwhelming debt, create financial ease, and achieve financial independence.

This rule has three guiding principles:

1. Take action to create change.

2. Simplicity and restraint create ease.

3. Consistent effort over time produces success.

I call it the Rule of 25. Here's how you can apply it.

Pay off your debt

If your debt is overwhelming, I have discovered that it's likely to equal 25 percent of one to two years of your household income. See for yourself. Add up your debt and divide it by your income.

Reduce your spending by 25 percent and use it to pay off your debt. You'll need to be aggressive, but it will be worth it. The goal is to be debt-free in 12 to 18 months. Remember, as you reduce spending, what you cut doesn't have to be gone forever, but it does have to be gone now so that you can be debt-free.

Save 25 percent

Once you achieve freedom from debt, continue to live on three-quarters of your income. Invest the remaining 25 percent to achieve financial independence.

Limit housing costs

If you are like most people, housing is your largest expense. If you limit your rent or mortgage to 25 percent of your income, you'll have money to save, spend, and give. Yes, you may have to give up some things you'd like to have in a house, or you may have to get a roommate, perhaps even two. However, you won't be house-poor.

Control your lifestyle

Lifestyle escalation can leave you feeling like you never make enough money. When you get a raise, add just 25 percent of it to your spending. Direct the remaining portion to your investment account. You won't miss what you didn't have, and your journey toward financial independence will accelerate over the years.

Save for 25 years

Saving 25 percent of your income for 25 years will leave you financially independent and free to work as you see fit. Consistent investing will have allowed you to dollar-cost-average – buying more stocks or mutual funds when the price is low and less when they are higher. Also, you'll avoid buying when the market is high and panic selling when it goes down.

By applying the Rule of 25, you can take control of your money and achieve financial independence.

29

Stories Of Success: Eliminate Debt And Build A Savings

For the last several months, I've discussed some of the tools essential to creating true financial independence. As you know, transforming your relationship with money is possible. With a goal and a plan, you can escape the trap of debt.

Today, I want to share a few success stories.

Debt-free during a recession

Even after the economy slipped into recession this single, 40-something, man was able to pay off his debt in 11 months. When we met, he had two credit cards with a combined balance of $3,900 and a looming $700 car repair bill. He owns a small business and earns $41,000 a year.

First, he divided his savings into a $1,000 emergency fund and an accumulation account with $700 for the car repairs and $400 for other expenses.

Next, he stopped using his credit cards, started paying an extra $325 a month toward those bills, and began budgeting each month for future purchases. These small changes allowed him to finish the year with no debt, a $1,000 emergency fund and nearly $2,300 in savings for future expenditures.

Cash equals peace of mind

This couple, in their mid-thirties with a three-year-old, now has a savings thanks to paying cash.

When we met, they were putting all of their monthly expenses on a credit card to acquire airline miles. At the end of each month, they paid off the balance on the card. They had no emergency fund or savings for future expenses.

Their monthly bill averaged about $2,000. In a year, this allowed them to accrue enough miles for one round-trip ticket. They intended to start saving, but each month, there always seemed to be an extra expense that prevented them from getting started.

After we discussed how credit-card use typically leads to overspending by 12 to 30 percent, they decided to stop using them and start using a budget and cash envelope system. Through the use of a budget, they reduced their spending by 15 percent – the changes came primarily in the areas of groceries, eating lunch out, and impulse clothing purchases.

The result was that one year later, they had saved $928 – enough to buy two round-trip tickets, and accumulated $2,000 in a savings account.

A budget tells the truth

Creating a budget allowed this couple to make some major changes.

Four years after buying their home, they had a home-equity line of credit nearly maxed out at $38,000.

By taking an honest inventory of their expenses, they realized they spent about $800 more each month than they earned. On "good months," they had about $200 left over. When "unexpected expenses" came along, they spent $150 to $1,500 more than they brought home.

After creating a budget, they practically eliminated "unexpected expenses" by planning for future expenses such as home improvement projects, car repairs, insurance, and holiday costs.

With a realistic budget in place, they decided to sell their house, pay off their line of credit, and purchase a less expensive home. Today, they are saving about $600 a month.

In each of these stories, change was possible after people became conscious of their spending habits and that their choices were costing them their dreams. Creating a budget and managing their cash flow allowed them to eliminate debt, build savings, and begin the journey toward their dreams.

30

SEX, MONEY AND GETTING ALONG WITH YOUR PARTNER

Sadly, a recent *Money Magazine* survey revealed 6 in 10 husbands and wives check their bank balances more often than they have sex.

Surprising? Not really. Seventy percent of couples said money causes most of their spats. Yes, finances are a more common source of disagreement and irritation than household chores, snoring or what's for dinner.

What's all this fighting about? The top four trouble spots are spending; saving; deceit; and exclusion from decisions. If these sound familiar, I have some strategies to help you stop fighting and start cooperating.

Spending

Frivolous spending is the incendiary behavior that ignites most arguments about how partners use – or misuse – their money. Men and women blame each other equally for careless spending.

To stop clashing over who is spending what, jointly develop a spending plan: create a budget, allocate spending money for each person and spend with integrity.

Your budget should account for:

- Basic necessities.
- Debts and other obligations.
- Expenses that occur less than monthly.
- Not-necessary, but nice-to-have items.

If you don't budget some money for discretionary spending, it's likely you would wind up spending anyway, and probably too much. So put it in your budget, then stop spending when you run out!

Stick to your plan – this is spending with integrity. Using a cash envelope will help you be accountable. When you decide how much discretionary spending fits into your monthly budget, put that amount in cash in an envelope for its designated purpose.

Saving

Thirty-seven percent of couples fight about saving money. In my experience, the lack of savings is a key cause of worries, fights, and sleepless nights.

Try these three tactics to save more and reduce your stress:

- Accumulate money for less-than-monthly expenses, such as tires, insurance, and holiday gifts.

- Build an emergency fund of at least $1,000. Once you are debt-free, increase the fund to equal three to six months of living expenses.

- With that foundation in the bank, put yourself on the path to financial independence by saving 15% of your take-home pay.

Deceit

Nearly 25 percent of those surveyed said they hid purchases and lied about how much money they spent. Why? Most wanted to avoid a fight or lecture.

By establishing a spending plan together, and spending with integrity, the perceived need for deceit should vanish.

Exclusion from decisions

For relationships to succeed, each person must have a voice in decision-making.

Dividing financial tasks based on each partner's interest is one of the best ways to create cooperation. For example, maybe one person loves spreadsheets and could tackle the budget, and the other likes to plan and could predict future spending needs.

However, the tasks are divided; both people need to participate, understand what choices are being made, and contribute to key decisions.

Choosing to work together will do wonders for bringing you closer to your partner.

31

Say 'I Do' to Talking About Money

Arguments about money are the top predictor of divorce.

Fights about kids, sex, in-laws or anything else for that matter take a back seat to money, says Sonya Britt, a researcher at Kansas State University. This is true for men and women, regardless of their income, debt, or net worth.

Her research also confirmed what you already might know: Arguments about money are more intense and last longer than other disagreements.

But conflict doesn't have to be inevitable. Healthy money communication with your spouse or partner may be easier than you think. Use these five steps to create an open dialogue, identify shared goals, and meet your individual needs:

Unpack you money beliefs

A period of quiet reflection will help clarify your beliefs and attitudes about money. With pen and paper in hand, spend about an hour journaling about these questions:

- When you think about money, what words come to mind?
- What does money mean for you?
- Who or what has influenced your financial decisions?
- When you think about how you handle money, what patterns do you see?

Now, ask your partner to do the same. Then set aside time to share your answers. Be open and honest. There are no right or wrong answers

Remove financial stress

Financial stress often leads to fights. Discuss your fears about money with one another. Then work together to remedy the situation. Even if your partner's fears seem trivial, address them.

Establish a common dream

Sharing a common dream – a big goal meaningful to both of you – will help you work as a team. By focusing on your dream, you will be able to say no to lesser desires that may be a source of conflict.

Get what you both want

Build a budget that expresses your shared values and priorities.

For example, in Step 1, you may have discovered money represents security for one of you and status for the other. Unacknowledged, these different values could lead to trouble. The solution is to craft a budget that saves money for security and sets aside money for spending on a status item.

Check in regularly

Don't let all of this effort go to waste. At least once a month, sit down and review your budget. What's working and what isn't? Ask your partner how he or she is feeling about your financial situation and what he or she would like to change.

Taking time to truly understand each other's beliefs about money and honoring those beliefs can keep you from becoming another divorce statistic.

32

SOLVE YOUR FINANCIAL DILEMMAS

Managing money can often seem like an endless series of choices between undesirable alternatives. And when a couple manages their money together, financial dilemmas have the potential to become permanent problems.

Let's consider this hypothetical complaint: "My husband wastes $400 a month on coffee and lunches out. What can I do?"

The dilemma? The wife sees her husband's purchases as a waste and feels his spending is depriving her of things she would like to do. The husband sees his purchases as necessary or allowable indulgences.

What is going on here and what can be done about it?

First, we must acknowledge reality. Every day we try to make ourselves happy. In our society, that often means buying things, but money is a finite resource. So saying "yes" to one purchase means saying "no" to another.

There is the dilemma: If the husband buys something to make him happy, then his wife cannot use that same money to purchase something to make her happy.

Can both husband and wife be happy when they have limited resources?

Yes, they can.

Through this four-step process, partners can structure their spending in a way that leads to mutual and individual happiness.

Find a shared dream

This dream could be a vacation, home improvements, starting a business, or raising children. Whatever it is, the dream must be shared, so both people are working toward an agreed upon goal. When a couple is not working toward a common goal, each person's happiness can come at the expense of the other's. A recipe for conflict.

Create a budget

Because every couple has a finite amount of money, they should aim to satisfy their needs and desires with the money available to them. By creating a budget, a couple can make a plan to spend only the money they have and save themselves from spending money they don't have.

Build in accountability

Discretionary spending is the most common source of fights about money. Using a cash-envelope system can allow a couple to spend with integrity and avoid conflicts similar to the one above.

When getting started, partners should agree on what spending will be done in cash and dedicate an envelope to each category. I recommend these categories:

- groceries
- restaurants
- entertainment
- spending money
- gasoline
- miscellaneous

Then, using their budget, they can take money out of each paycheck to fill the envelopes.

Have spending money

Make sure to include spending money as a cash envelope – one for each partner. Spending money is cash each person can spend in any way that makes him or her happy without being accountable to the other.

With a shared dream, a budget, financial integrity, and some spending money, financial dilemmas and fights over money can disappear.

33

In A Relationship, Separate Finances Signal Trouble

Couples who choose to manage their money separately are at risk for both financial and relationship trouble.

Some couples say they maintain independent accounts because one person is a spender or because they have different views on money management and debt. Some do it simply because it's easier.

I know this story. My wife, Cheri, and I kept separate checking accounts for many years. In fact, our banks in Chicago merged before we merged our accounts. We told ourselves this approach was easier.

But the truth is individual accounts can signal a lack of shared priorities. The independence that once seemed so convenient may end up eroding trust between partners. Without financial cooperation, real problems can begin to weaken a couple's bond.

The fallout from unresolved money issues drives a wedge between partners. Fifty-seven percent of divorced couples in the United States say financial problems are the primary reason for their split, according to a Citibank survey.

Independent spending can push couples apart as each person sees the other as an obstacle to achieving his or her goals. Whatever the motivations may be for keeping finances separate, the solution is the same: create shared dreams and goals and begin living on a budget that reflects those priorities.

Establishing common financial goals is a challenging process, but it can be richly rewarding. To get started, I encourage you and your partner to spend an afternoon finding your shared dream. This can be done by dreamstorming, creating a vision board, or simply talking openly and honestly.

Begin by understanding what you value as an individual. Then combine your values with your partner's to create a mutual dream to serve as your motivation and compass. This goal will help you measure whether your new approach to money management is successful.

Now it's time to create a budget, which will help you spend in alignment with your priorities. Co-creating a realistic budget and holding yourselves accountable are the keys to success. Remember, a realistic budget accounts not only for your immediate needs but also your future needs.

Because you do not have an unlimited stream of income, you will need to decide how to allocate your money to satisfy your variety of needs. Compromise is essential. Your budget should reflect this and be specific about how to meet your individual and mutual needs, including, accumulating money to meet your shared dream.

But it's not enough to create your budget and leave it. A budget won't do the work for you. It must be a living document that changes month to month and even at times week to week to address the reality of your situation. Unexpected expenses, undisciplined spending, and – hooray! – unexpected income must all be accounted for to stay on course toward your goal.

Managing your money together can be a challenge, but it has the potential to reduce financial stress and let you and your partner build more than your bank accounts.

34

WARNING: DON'T MAKE THE SAME MISTAKES I DID

Alaina Tweddale of the personal finance website Wise Bread recently interviewed me about how my wife, Cheri, and I paid off $165,000 in debt and saved $20,000 in just 15 months.

When our discussion turned to the topic of "what I wish I'd known then that I know now," I knew this edition of Money Savvy would be about avoiding the money mistakes I made.

Let me go back to the beginning of our story. When Cheri and I decided to get married, I was a young entrepreneur financing my start-up software company with credit cards.

Mistake 1: Over three years, I had maxed out two credit cards, totaling about $10,000 in debt.

Lesson: I should have continued to live as I did in graduate school when I took a full load of classes, studied like mad, and worked weekends as a bartender.

I relied on credit cards and debt because I was taking home only $12,000 to $18,000 annually. If I had picked up a part-time job when I started my company, I could have lived frugally and relied on the extra income instead of my credit cards.

Mistake 2: We never discussed our money beliefs or our spending habits, and we didn't consider getting any help with our finances.

Lesson: When we were making significant financial decisions that would affect us long-term, we needed the guidance of a personal finance professional.

In the year before Cheri and I were married, my income had risen dramatically. That, combined with Cheri's income, allowed us to qualify for a mortgage. We closed on a condo in the weeks before our wedding.

To do so, we sold the small stock portfolio Cheri's grandfather had started for her. With the proceeds, we paid off my credit card debt and put a small down payment on the condo.

We made two major financial decisions – selling a significant asset and making a major purchase – without talking about our personal finances. We should have sought help from a personal finance professional. We didn't, and 18 months later, we had accumulated $18,000 in credit card debt.

Although we paid off the $18,000 by selling our first condo and were able to buy a larger condo in an up-and-coming neighborhood, we didn't change our behavior.

Mistake 3: Over and over again, we ran up credit card debt and rolled it into our mortgage.

Lesson: We were trading our dreams for debt.

We were caught in a cycle of unconscious spending, unaware that we were making choices that were steering us away from our dreams. Had we been more intentional and explicit about our choices – saying "yes" to one option and "no" to another – I believe we could have avoided the trap of unconscious spending.

Ultimately, the big lesson is about choice. We must step back from our everyday lives and examine our choices honestly. How are we choosing to live and spend our money? Are those choices helping us realize our dreams? If not, it's time to change course and move toward our goals.

35

Teach Your Children Well: Save, Give, Spend

The beliefs, behaviors, and habits we develop about money during our childhood can last a lifetime. For better or worse, they can affect our attitudes about spending and saving as adults.

Parents and role models can help children develop a healthy relationship with money from an early age. My wife and I have successfully used a simple system to teach our son how to manage the money he earns at home.

Our approach grows out of the primary ways we handle our money: saving, spending, and giving. Once your kids are old enough to do some simple work around the house, this system can give them a solid foundation for developing money skills. We started when Malcolm was five years old.

The three principles of this system are:

1. Pay a commission for work done.

2. Divide the commission into three envelopes: save, give, and spend.

3. Fines inappropriate behavior are paid out of the commission.

Get started by explaining to your children they have the opportunity to earn some money, learn how to handle it responsibly and make some decisions of their own along the way.

Introduce the three envelopes to make the system more concrete. The save envelope is for future purchases; the giving envelope is for charitable donations of their choice, and the spending envelope is for buying personal items. Help your kids pick a savings goal – something that will take at least a few weeks to save for so they can learn about delayed gratification.

Your children will be earning the commission, so together choose three to five tasks for which they will be paid. Also, identify three to five unpaid tasks they will be responsible for as a family member.

Pick age-appropriate jobs and commissions; don't forget to set expectations about how and when the tasks will be completed. For example, cleaning their rooms may be something they are expected to do without pay, but helping with laundry is paid work.

Fines are used to give inappropriate behavior tangible consequences. You and your children, for example, might pick arguing as a 50-cent fine and hitting as $1 fine. At this stage, it's important to let your children help with identifying inappropriate behavior – they know what bothers you and what the house rules are. They also should help set the amount of the fines.

Commission, minus any fines, should be paid weekly or on another consistent interval. And commissions should be divided into the three envelopes.

Our son must put at least a dollar in each of the three envelopes, provided he has earned at least three dollars. Any money beyond the three dollars goes into envelopes of his choosing.

Our experience with this system has been wonderful. I see Malcolm learning how to handle his money responsibly. He is generous in his giving, proud of himself after saving for a big purchase and is a cautious shopper after making some poor buying decisions. I think he's off to a great start.

36

HELP YOUR TEEN MANAGE MONEY WISELY

The sooner teenagers begin to learn smart money management; the sooner they can become financially independent adults.

Right now, 57 percent of all 20-year-olds are dependent on their families for financial support, according to an American Express survey. Or, to put it another way, a majority of parents who have a child in his or her 20s are helping pay their child's bills.

Today, I want to share three methods for creating money-savvy teens and, I hope, financially independent young adults.

Begin with a budget

I believe the habit of building and using a budget is an essential life skill. Help your teenager learn this habit.

Teens have expenses, and a budget can help them understand and organize those expenses. Use the money you spend on clothing and activities to create a budget, and then turn the money over to your teen.

With a plan in hand, your child can spend the money. This is an opportunity to learn how to shop wisely.

I'm not suggesting you hand over your credit card. Rather, decide how much you can afford to put toward school needs, activities, and social life and consider that money "income." At first, help your child create a spending plan, and, later, have them create the plan and present it to you.

If your teen has a job, his or her income should be factored into the budget.

Start a mini-emergency fund

When getting started managing money, budgets are fragile, and a crisis can quickly sink your teenager's plans. The goal for your child – and you too – is to have three to six months of living expenses in an emergency fund.

When your child is getting started, the fund can be modest, and you can help build it.

I suggest you match your teen dollar for dollar to help them reach the goal more quickly. Most banks require $100 to open a savings account. So challenge your child to save $50 and match it with $50. Then go to the bank together to open the fund.

Now set a new goal of reaching an amount equal to three months of the budget. Encourage your teen to save a little each month to meet that goal.

Avoid student loan debt

College graduates are leaving school with an average of $23,000 in student loan debt.

Your child's senior year of high school is not the best time to start researching scholarships. Ideally, you will start when your teenager enters ninth grade.

Make the most of the high school's resources and online resources when scholarship hunting. A quick search on www.FinAid.org shows scholarships of $10,000, $25,000 and $50,000. Carefully review the eligibility requirements of possible scholarships so your teen can build a foundation to be competitive in the race for tuition money and reduce reliance on student loans.

You can put your teen on the path to financial health and independence with these three strategies. After all, The Bank of Mom and Dad can't stay open forever.

37

NAVIGATING THE ODYSSEY ON THE WAY TO ADULTHOOD

Our world is evolving faster than ever. The economy, technology, and culture drive changes in our lives at a remarkable pace and in unpredictable ways.

In the past, lives could be defined by four distinct phases: childhood, adolescence, adulthood, and old age. Today, two more phases come into play: the odyssey and active retirement.

The odyssey has emerged as the period of wandering many 20-somethings experience between adolescence and adulthood. During this time, traditional markers of adulthood, such as marriage and career, are delayed, replaced by a period of searching and experimentation.

The uncertainty of these years leads many people to move back home with mom and dad. In her book *Slouching Toward Adulthood: Observations from the Not-So-Empty Nest,* Sally Koslow says nearly 6 million adults ages 20 to 35 are living at home.

What's the reason for this new life phase? Changes in the economy and work culture are the likely forces driving this epic journey from adolescence to adulthood.

At the height of the industrial economy in the 1960s, the typical 30-year-old had fully reached adulthood, having moved away from home, secured a "good" job, married and had children. The formula was: get good grades, go to college, get a job that leads to a career, and live happily ever after. It worked – back then.

Today, as we move into the connection economy, the certainty of that formula is gone. Good grades and a college degree are no longer a sure ticket to a stable economic livelihood.

What are parents to do?

For those of us who are late baby boomers and Generation X'ers with children, we must prepare for their odyssey by:

- Talking with them about the connection economy.
- Preparing financially for the odyssey years.
- Setting healthy boundaries.

The connection economy

Even though following the old formula won't guarantee success, education remains crucial. It can help your children meet the demands of the new economy, which requires applying what we know in ways that inspire a connection between people, evoke emotions, cause them to tell stories and dream.

113

Our children will need to learn to thrive as independent artists, as freelancers – not as employees for life. Trying new endeavors, being creative, and discovering opportunities in unexpected places will lead them to success.

The financial odyssey

The majority of young adults receive financial assistance from their parents during these years, says Patrick Wrightman of the University of Michigan. The average amount of assistance totals about $7,500. Parents need to be prepared for this financial reality.

Just as you are saving for your child's college education, you may want to save for your child's odyssey years. But one caution: Don't sacrifice your financial security to support post-college-age children.

Healthy boundaries

Assisting adult children financially can lead to conflicts between couples – especially in second marriages involving stepchildren. You and your partner must decide together how to spend your collective money. Yes, I'm talking about budgeting and planning.

As with all financial commitments, preparation is essential.

38

READY TO BUY A HOME? TAKE A REALITY CHECK(LIST) FIRST

With headlines like "Mortgage rates are falling again" and "Home sales begin to rebound," you may be hearing the call to homeownership.

Yes, it is a good time to buy: Mortgage rates are hovering near record lows, and home prices have begun to stabilize after dropping as much as 40 percent in some areas during the last five years.

But is it a good time for *you* to buy? Achieving the dream of homeownership involves more than favorable interest rates and a promising market. You need to assess your financial readiness. That's the real test.

These two simple checklists can help you make a decision. They will tell you if you are ready to buy and what your limits are when shopping and negotiating.

Personal finances

- Do you have and use a written budget? A realistic budget – with actual numbers – will let you know if buying a home is a smart decision. Your budget should include monthly payment obligations, future expenses, and nice-to-have items. Be comprehensive and be honest with yourself.

- Do you have debt – car loans, credit cards, or personal loans? If you do, now is the time to focus on paying off that debt instead of buying a home. A house will come with many expenses you don't have when you rent. Debts may get in the way of handling home maintenance.

- Do you have an emergency fund? An emergency fund equal to three to six months of living expenses – usually $10,000-$20,000 – will give you peace of mind and financial stability if your income is interrupted. This is not down-payment money.

Eliminating debt and having an emergency fund will not only make homeownership a possibility; it can make it a joy.

Home affordability

- A 20 percent down payment in the bank. Your down payment should be no less than 20 percent of the purchase price. If you put down less, you will likely be paying private mortgage insurance, often called PMI. This typically costs between 0.5 and 1 percent of the purchase price annually. On a $200,000 home, for example, PMI will add about $166 to each monthly payment. Not a small amount and these payments last at least five years.

- Monthly house payment. This number – called PITI – calculates principle, interest, property taxes, and insurance. Ideally, the total should land somewhere between 25 percent and 30 percent of household take-home pay. By keeping payments in this safe zone, you will be prepared to deal with life's challenges and enjoy homeownership.

- Deferred maintenance and repairs. There is more to homeownership than making the monthly house payment. You must plan for maintenance and improvements. Before buying, have a professional assess what maintenance will need to be done within the next five years so you can budget for it. A good monthly estimate of maintenance costs is one-tenth of 1 percent of the purchase price. The maintenance budget on a $200,000 home would be about $200 a month.

The affordability checklist should drive your price-range considerations, offer, and negotiating.

Following these guidelines can allow you to own your home happily rather than having the home own you. Good luck.

39

Buying A Home? Make Sure You're Truly Ready

You've heard the clichés about homeownership: It makes financial sense to own instead of rent. It's one of the best investments you can make. It's the American dream!

Buying your first home can be a rite of passage into adulthood, a symbol of financial maturity and independence. But how do you know if it's the right time to buy? Is your decision based on the numbers – income, debt, interest rates, current home values?

Sure, these numbers may add up for you, but your decision should be based on more than numbers alone. Consider your financial mindset. Do you have control over your budget, spending, and debt? Are you living with the financial discipline that can make owning a home a joy rather than a burden?

Mortgage lenders will help you with the numbers, but don't expect them to have your back. It's not their job.

When you meet with a lender, you'll need to answer these questions.

- How much do you want to spend on a house?
- How much money do you have for a down payment?
- How much money do you make?
- Have you been at your current job for more than two years?
- How much debt do you have?

Lenders typically use the 28/36 rule. They want your mortgage payment – often called PITI for principal, interest, taxes, and insurance – to be no greater than 28 percent of your gross monthly income.

The more money you have for a down payment, the more expensive the home you can buy and remain under the 28 percent guideline. Be aware that buyers with less than a 20 percent down payment will need to pay private mortgage insurance.

The 36 percent of the 28/36 rule indicates the maximum amount of debt you can assume as a percent of your monthly income when including your mortgage. For example, a buyer with a gross income of $75,000 a year could spend $2,250 on debt each month, with not more than $1,750 (28 percent) of the $2,250 (36 percent) dedicated to a mortgage.

In Durango, the median home price in the first quarter of 2014 was $338,000. This means a buyer with a gross income of $75,000 and a 20 percent down payment ($67,600) could expect a monthly mortgage payment of $1,735 (based on a 4.25 percent mortgage rate).

This barely fits within the 28 percent of the 28/36 rule. That was Cheri and me with our first condo. Going by the numbers only, we completely missed considering our financial mindset, overlooking the keys to making owning a home a rewarding experience.

Before talking numbers with a lender, consider these key principles:

- Live by a realistic, written budget for a year.
- Use the envelope system for discretionary spending.
- Cut up your credit cards.
- Be debt free before you buy.
- Have an emergency fund equal to three to six months of living expenses.

If you follow these rules, you'll find that you are prepared to enjoy the blessings of a home and handle the burdens.

40

CAUTION! LIFESTYLE INFLATION AHEAD

I had to issue that warning to myself yesterday. I love looking at big, old homes and imagining what it would be like to live there.

Spring has sprung here in Philadelphia, and I've been exploring the neighborhoods. Recently, in my mind, I moved into a coach house big enough for three families and a mansion built in 1752, nearly 130 years before Durango was on the map. With each move, of course, came the inflated lifestyle to match.

Lifestyle inflation

Lifestyle inflation, or lifestyle creep, is the tendency to spend more as we earn more. We can also inflate our lifestyle after we pay off debts and then spend that money unconsciously.

Increased spending is not always a bad thing. It's perfectly natural to want a more comfortable lifestyle as your income increases. After all, the living conditions of our college years aren't meant to last forever. But left unchecked, lifestyle inflation can trade our future for today's desires.

121

Audit your lifestyle

I suggest checking for lifestyle creep every year, right after you finish your taxes. Review your finances in these five areas:

Your budget: Do you have and follow a budget that includes accumulating money for less-than-monthly expenses? If your answer is "no," create one.

Bank and credit card statements: Look for luxuries, indulgences, overspending and recurring charges on these statements. This is an opportunity to eliminate waste. When I reviewed my statements, I found a gym membership that had continued to bill us after cancellation.

Housing costs: Calculate the percentage of your take-home pay that you spend on housing. If it's more than 35 percent, your lifestyle today may harm your future. Also, review how much it costs to maintain your home. Some of the old homes I've looked at come with a budget-busting number of renovation projects.

Debt: If you have consumer debt, such as credit cards, car payments, or a personal loan, it's a symptom of living beyond your income. Total your balances and divide that number by 12 or 18 months. That's the amount you'll need to pay off each month to be debt-free next year.

Emergency fund: If you are debt-free, congratulations! Now, do you have an emergency fund equal to three to six months of living expenses? If not, it's time to build one by redirecting lifestyle spending into your savings account.

Don't delay action

Being debt-free, having an emergency fund, and saving at least 15 percent of your income is a clear indication that your lifestyle is congruent with your earning power.

If your audit revealed areas where you need to make changes to reach these goals, take action right now. Like pulling off a Band-Aid, quick is best.

41

PROFESSOR NUDGE SAYS: AUTOMATE YOUR SAVINGS!

In my last column, I warned about the hazards of lifestyle inflation. Today, I'll give you a few tools to prevent spending more than you earn and start automatically saving for your future.

Lifestyle inflation can creep up on us, especially after we pay off debts and feel like there's extra, "free" money in our budget. This tendency to increase spending can compromise our retirement, financial goals, and dreams.

Saving money shouldn't be an exercise in willpower with every paycheck. That's asking too much.

With that in mind, I turned to Professor Nudge, Richard Thaler, for solutions. Thaler, author of *Nudge: Improving Decisions about Health, Wealth and Happiness*, offers this lesson in behavioral economics: "… people only save if it's automatic. If people just put away what's left at the end of the month, that's a recipe for failure."

Thanks to technology, automating your savings is easier than ever. Here are a few apps that can do the work of building your savings, and if the idea of combining technology and money unsettles you, I've got a DIY solution, too.

- Clarity Money, https://claritymoney.com, can automate your savings and suggest ways to eliminate overspending by, for example, canceling unused recurring charges, such as the gym membership you don't use.

- Digit, https://digit.co, automates your savings by learning your habits and trying to move money daily from your checking account to your Digit account. Don't worry: They are so confident in the app's ability to not overdraft your account they'll pay the overdraft fee if it happens.

- Rize, https://rizemoney.com, is on a mission to help you eliminate spending more than you make. Rize automates saving and pays an interest rate on that savings to help accelerate you toward your goals. Plus, Rize is building a community of support to foster conversations about money.

- Stash, https://stashinvest.com, is an automated investment platform that allows you to start investing with as little as $5 and build over time. Stash offers a variety of portfolio options and personalized guidance.

- Finally, the DIY option. Open a savings account at your bank and set up a monthly automatic transfer of funds, a "nudge," from your checking account. You'll save before you even knew the money was in your account by setting the transfer date for the day after you get paid.

There are many more automatic saving and investing options, thanks to the proliferation of smartphones and decision-making algorithms. Choose one that works for you and start building your savings.

Whatever you choose, take this advice from Professor Nudge:

- Get off your ass and start saving.
- Save more tomorrow and ramp it up one or two percentage points a year until you are at least up to 12 percent.
- Invest using a diversified portfolio.

42

A HOLIDAY BUDGET CAN BE THE BEST GIFT OF ALL

The bright colors of autumn have faded, and already snow has fallen in town. The sun is setting early, and the nights are cold. The holidays are nearly upon us.

This week tables will be set for Thanksgiving dinner, but the holiday season won't end until New Year's – almost six weeks from now. There are meals to make, gifts to buy, and relatives to visit. The holidays can be a stressful and expensive time.

Don't let money worries be the coal in your stocking this year. With your finances under control, you can spend your time celebrating, rather than sweating the bottom line.

Reducing stress always starts with good planning. Last-minute decisions tend to be expensive ones. Get your holiday plans in order now. What are you doing for Thanksgiving? How are you going to celebrate Hanukkah or Christmas? What about New Year's Eve?

Map out a realistic budget that fits your finances, and match it up against your plans. If you find your holiday fund comes up short, adjust your plans, or get creative with ways to raise and save money.

Three quick ways to boost your budget:

- Sell things you don't need anymore on eBay, Craigslist or through classifieds ads.
- Try using coupons to save money on your grocery bills. Put the money you save toward holiday gatherings and gifts. Try CouponMom.com, which includes how-to tips and links to coupons.
- Sell the gold from old or broken jewelry, or sell old cell phones and gadgets you no longer use. As always, make sure you take precautions to avoid scams – check out the tips on the National Consumers League's website www.fraud.org.

As fun as holiday meals can be to share, preparing them for a large group can quickly become time consuming and expensive. To minimize stress and save money, ask friends and family to make your holiday meals potlucks. This way, you won't have to bear the financial burden of an elaborate meal, and a potluck gives everyone a chance to share his or her favorite recipes.

Gift giving, of course, can be the most costly aspect of the season. An afternoon of last-minute shopping has the potential to leave your budget in tatters.

With your immediate family, set a limit and stick to it. Feeling like you want to give more? Try handmade gifts or creating personal coupons good for everyday chores and special treats. A handmade gift or the gift of time can carry more value than a store-bought item. If you are gathering with extended family, instead of buying gifts for everyone, try drawing names and setting a limit on the gift's price.

The next six weeks don't have to be a financial obstacle course if you set expectations now. You may even discover friends and family appreciate you making the holidays more about relationships and time together and less about buying and spending. It's not too late to give yourself the gift of peace of mind.

43

TIME TO PREPARE FOR THE HOLIDAYS – YES, IT REALLY IS

When kids returned to school this week, I suspect you were as shocked as me. How did the summer fly by so quickly? Knowing that the busyness of school and work will accelerate life, I decided to look ahead.

I turned my calendar to the holidays. We have only 126 days until Christmas and 98 days until the start of Hanukkah. Even though you may not be finished with back-to-school expenses, now is the time to think about budgeting for the holiday season. Yes, it really is.

The typical U.S. family spent about $850 on the holidays last year, according to the American Research Group. If you were to budget and save throughout the year, you would need to save $71 a month to achieve that goal.

If you haven't been setting aside that $71 a month? Here's a plan to prepare you for the holidays or any future expense.

You'll be saving a portion of your holiday money each time you get paid during the next 16 weeks. First, consider how much discretionary money you have during that time.

Next, plan your holiday experience by creating a budget for meals, parties, gifts, and charitable donations. Compare this total to how much you can easily save. If it's less, you're in the clear.

If the amount you budgeted exceeds the amount you can easily save, something has to give. Either you need to cut back on your holiday expenses, or you need to cut back your spending now so you can have what you want later. This is the essence of budgeting and planning.

Some ideas to consider if your budget was in the red:

- Remove a few luxuries from your monthly budget until you reach your goal.
- Consider selling some items you no longer need. Ebay, Craigslist, and fall garage sales are quick ways to turn unwanted items into cash.
- Apply for a part-time job this fall. Businesses may be adding staff members to meet holiday demands.

Once you start saving, you need to keep the money safe. Temptation and easy access to your savings can thwart a good plan.

Your parents or grandparents may have had a Christmas club account at a local bank or savings and loan where they deposited a little bit of money each week to use at holiday time. This simple and effective method of building a nest egg can work for any goal.

Christmas club accounts reached the height of their popularity in the 1970s. They were simple savings accounts with restrictions that encouraged regular saving and infrequent withdrawals.

Today, with $100 saved, you can open a separate account to serve as your special savings fund – whether it's for the holidays, a vacation, or any other savings goal.

School has started, signs of autumn are in the air and, before you know it, the holidays will be upon us. Begin saving today.

44

THE HOLIDAYS DON'T HAVE TO BE STRESSFUL

Just when you thought life was stressful enough – work, parenting, an overbooked schedule – the holidays arrive.

Parties, gift-buying, and family gatherings can add additional layers of stress to your life. When visions of the "perfect holiday" run into the reality of our day-to-day lives and finances, we can become cranky and anxious.

The leading holiday stressors, according to a study by Greenberg Quinlan Rosner Research, are:

- lack of time
- lack of money
- hype and commercialism

But you can get through the holidays without feeling overwhelmed. By practicing healthy budgeting and using the WISE checklist, you can transform your stress into joy.

First, prepare a holiday budget: Determine how much you can spend without damaging other financial goals and obligations. Then, based on what you can spend, allocate money to these categories: gifts, charitable giving, food, decorations, travel, and a holiday emergency fund. This fund should equal 10 to 20 percent of what you have to spend and give you a cushion for handling forgotten or unexpected expenses.

Next, budget your time:

- How much vacation time do you have available?
- If you have kids, what's their holiday schedule?
- Will you have guests visiting or be traveling?
- What activities do you want to do so the holidays feel special?
- How much time will be required for shopping, decorating, and cooking?

Using your answers, build a rough schedule. Do it in pencil because changes are likely. Try scheduling only 40 percent of your available time with things that must be done. This way, you can take advantage of unexpected opportunities or meet unexpected obligations.

With your financial and time budgets in place, you are ready to use the WISE checklist to handle the holidays' hype and commercialism.

When you start feeling stressed or become aware that you are piling on more spending, tasks, and commitments than feel comfortable; review the checklist:

- Wherewithal: Do you have the time and money required?

- Integrity: Will you be giving up things you value more by saying "yes"?

- Superhero: Do you believe you can, or have to, do it all?

- Elation: How are you feeling? Will saying "yes" contribute to more joy or more stress?

By using these tools, you can make the holidays a season of joy.

45

WHAT'S THE REAL COST OF YOUR DEBT?

A few days ago, I was discussing debt with a new client. The interest payments were killing him.

He repeatedly said that they were his primary motivation for getting out of debt. Then I asked him, "What are the other costs of having debt?"

He was unable to come up with an answer. I suspect he's not alone.

What's your answer? How do you calculate the cost of your debt?

I measure the cost in several ways: financial, emotional, physical, and spiritual. Yes, even spiritual. More on that later.

Financial cost

Interest expense is the most obvious cost of being in debt, but it's not the only financial cost. When we are in debt, we also lose the opportunity to invest the money we are paying the lender. It's a double-whammy.

The power of compound interest – the force that Albert Einstein called the "Eighth Wonder of the World" – can work for you or against you. Imagine if those interest payments were making you money rather than the lender.

Emotional cost

Unlike an interest payment, the emotional cost of debt is not fixed. Depending on your circumstances, it can vary – widely.

If your debt is manageable, such as a mortgage that requires a monthly payment that is 25 percent of your take-home pay or less, the emotional cost is likely to be low.

However, if your debt load reaches a level that makes you stressed and fearful, the emotional cost can take a serious toll. Add a partner to the mix, and you could find that one of you is tolerant of debt, and the other is not. Such differences can result in fights over money that exact an even higher cost.

Physical cost

Not only does constant worry tax us emotionally, but it can also wear us down physically. Long-term debt can mean long-term stress.

Chronic stress can manifest as chronic health problems, such as heart disease, high blood pressure, obesity, or diabetes. All of which add to your financial burden, creating a vicious circle.

Spiritual cost

Spirituality can be defined in many ways. For our discussion today, I'm using it to mean living your true purpose and serving those you are meant to serve.

Debt can be an obstacle to achieving these deeply fulfilling personal goals. Debt can leave you stuck in a job you don't love and drain you of the energy and drive to pursue your true calling. If this is the case, you are giving up your life for debt.

Yes, the cost of debt reaches far beyond that next interest payment. How is it affecting you?

46

IS THERE A MONSTER IN YOUR MAILBOX?

Are you scared to open your credit card bill, or should I say bills? The typical credit card user has four credit cards in his wallet.

If you are scared, you're not alone. Having had more than ten credit cards at one time and having been petrified at the sight of the bills, I know how it feels. Each trip to get the mail left me filled with worry and fear. It was like there was a monster living in my mailbox.

The worry and fear caused me to stop dreaming. That's the real problem with debt and unconscious spending – it steals dreams.

Ready for some good news? You can eliminate worry and fear this month and be debt free by this time next year!

Eliminate fear

I've learned that fear comes from the belief that something terrible is going to happen. In this case, the bad we're talking about is not being able to pay our bills, defaulting on loans and bankruptcy. If you're like me, you may be imagining a situation that is much worse than reality.

It's time to confront reality by adding up your debt. Gather all of your credit card, car loan, home equity line of credit and other loan statements, except for your mortgage. List the balances and minimum payments on a sheet of paper, or in a spreadsheet, from smallest to largest.

After working with lots of clients, I have learned that your total debt is likely to equal 25 percent of one to two years of your household income. See for yourself. Add up your debt and divide it by your income.

Attack those debts

Congratulations! You confronted the monster in the mailbox and lived to tell about it.

Now that you have a list of debts, you can start taking action. Pay the minimum payment on all of your debts except for the smallest one on your list. Attack that smallest debt like your dreams depend on it because they do.

Slay the monster

Reduce your spending and use it to pay off your debt. You'll need to be aggressive, but it will be worth it. Remember, as you cut expenses out of your budget, they don't have to be gone forever, but they do have to be gone for now so that you can become debt-free.

Paying off your debt can be hard, but along the way, you will take back control of your life and your dreams. You'll find that once you are committed, you will begin to notice all kinds of opportunities to chip away at the debt that is on top of your list.

Next, we'll explore how to accelerate paying off your debt.

47

FIVE KEYS TO ELIMINATING YOUR DEBT

Today's column is about getting started on a successful path to paying off your debt.

If you're like me, making more money isn't the only answer. After all, over the years, our income went up, and so did our debt. Reducing spending helps, but it can be hard to maintain willpower. We'd start and then revert to old habits in a few months.

Here's what we did, and I've seen it work for others, too.

Get organized

Our finances were out of control. Symptomatic of our state of mind, our bills and credit card statements were scattered in different spots around the house.

The first step toward paying off our debt was getting organized. Start with three file folders:

1. To Be Paid: As bills and credit card statements arrive in the mail, open them, and place them in this folder.

2. Paid Bills: When you pay a bill, move the statement to this folder. There is no need to have a folder for each type of bill you receive. Just put them all in one.

3. Paid Debts: Keep your debt statements separate from your monthly bills by placing them in a separate folder. This will make them easier for you to find.

Write it down

The truth is I didn't know how much debt we were in until I added it all up. As bad as it was, the fear of not knowing was worse.

With your statements organized, make a list of your debts from smallest to largest balance. Don't include your mortgage. Focus on credit cards, consumer debt, and other loans. For each, note the current balance and minimum payment due. You've now created your debt payoff worksheet.

Start small

Focus all of your effort on paying off the smallest debt on your list. Don't be tempted to pay a little extra on all of your debts. Pay off the smallest one ASAP.

Celebrate wins

A client reminded me about celebrating. I'm often so focused on fixing problems and setting goals that I forget to acknowledge small successes.

Each time you pay off a debt, cross it off of your debt-payoff worksheet and do something small to celebrate. It could be a pizza and movie night or going out for ice cream. Any small reward will work.

Look for opportunities

As you eliminate a small debt or two, you'll likely feel a surge of motivation. With that newfound money motivation, start looking for opportunities to reduce your debt. Get creative.

Success begets success. Take those small wins and build on them.

48

FOUND: MONEY! SAVE? SPEND? WHAT DO I DO?

"Matt, what would you recommend I do with my tax refund?"

At this time of year, I hear this question a lot. My answer: "It depends. Let me explain."

What you should do depends on where you are on your path to financial independence.

Whatever the source of "found" money may be – a tax refund, inheritance or simply an unexpected, fortunate event – you can use this guide to manage that money wisely and avoid the temptation to splurge.

Pay the bills

If you have past due bills, use all of your available resources to pay them off. Resist that urge to spend your found money on a vacation or ski trip and use it to get caught up.

You also might consider selling items you no longer need on Craig's List, eBay or Amazon. This is an easy way to raise a little extra cash for bill paying and clear out the clutter in your life.

Save for upcoming expenses

Don't let a pending expense become an emergency. Saving money for those less-than-monthly expenses is what makes a budget realistic and emergencies less likely.

Financial emergencies are often the result of a planning failure. Take car tires, for example. Frequently, purchasing them becomes a crisis, despite knowing they will wear out and need replacement. Ideally, you should accumulate a little money each month and be prepared for that expense when it comes.

Consider using your found money to establish an accumulation account to avoid this type of financial emergency. Don't let those less-than-monthly expenses turn into unwanted debts.

Create an emergency fund

Do you have at least a $1,000 tucked away for that unexpected emergency? If you don't, begin building an emergency fund. Do this before dedicating your found money to paying off debt.

Begin by saving $1,000. If your household income is less than $25,000, establish a $500 emergency fund. This extra cash will help you avoid taking on debt when the inevitable unexpected event happens.

146

Tackle that debt

Make a list – from smallest to largest – of all your non-mortgage-related debts, writing the exact amount owed to each creditor. Pay at least the minimum amount on each, and use your found money to eliminate as many debts as possible. For most people, the process of becoming debt-free takes just 12 to 18 months.

Grow your emergency fund

Once you've eliminated your non-mortgage debt, it's time to build your emergency fund from $1,000 to three to six months of living expenses. Yes, this requires a realistic budget to calculate. To make building your fund easier, dedicate the money that you were using to pay off debt to growing your emergency fund. Typically, this step takes about 12 months.

This year, use that tax refund to begin or advance your journey to financial independence. In just two years, you can go from broke and hoping your money lasts until your next paycheck to financially secure and prepared for financial success.

Make that found money work for you.

49

PLAN WISELY FOR YOUR REMARKABLE MOMENTS

Fill in the blank: Your best _____ ever!

What did you say? Was is it vacation, Thanksgiving, Christmas, Hanukkah or a long-dreamed-of adventure?

There is no right answer here. Consider your response a "remarkable moment" – these are the moments we tell stories about, the moments that provide enduring joy and connection. I want to help you get the most out them.

Too often, I see remarkable moments become sources of stress and financial panic. This anxiety drains the pleasure from what should be a fulfilling, memorable experience. Let's discover how to minimize that stress so you can truly enjoy the moment.

Typically, there are three ways people react to remarkable moments:

1. They reject the opportunity, saying they can't afford it.

2. They jump at the chance regardless of the cost.

3. They plan how to make the most of the opportunity without breaking the bank.

No. 1 can lead to regret, and No. 2 can lead to trouble. No. 3 is the path to fulfillment.

You can make the most of the opportunities in your life with these simple steps.

Step 1: Assess the opportunity by answering three questions:

- Do I want to devote my time, energy, and money to this opportunity?
- What will I have to give up to make this a remarkable moment?
- Given what I will have to give up, do I want to do it?

Step 2: If you choose to pursue the experience, develop a simple budget to determine how much it will cost.

Step 3: Compare this budget to your available resources. Do you have enough money saved?

Step 4: If you need to save more money, you have three options:

1. Divide the amount you must save by the number of months until the event, then save that amount each month.

2. Reduce your budget by limiting your expenses.

3. Earn some additional money. Consider taking on extra hours at work, getting a part-time job temporarily, or selling some things you no longer use.

Frequently, a combination of reducing your expenses and saving and earning a little extra money is the most effective way to reach your goal.

Step 5: Enjoy! You are responsibly pursuing a peak experience. By building a budget and accumulating money in advance, you are more likely to enjoy the moment and reap long-lasting benefits.

These simple steps are tools to reach your goals. My hope is that you make the most of the opportunities in your life.

And, how did I fill in that blank at the top? The Christmas holidays. My sister and her family are coming to Durango. I'm already planning for their visit. I can't wait.

50

Simple Strategies To Save For Your Next Vacation

My partner, Cheri, texted me a page from a Life Hack daily calendar with the premise that if Americans weren't too lazy to cook, we could afford plane tickets to exotic travel destinations.

Good idea for a column, right. With some research, here's what I discovered.

According to the Bureau of Labor Statistics, the average American household annually spends:

- $4,049 or $337/month on food at home.
- $3,154 or $263/month on food away from home.
- $2,913 or $243/month on entertainment.

That's a total of $10,116, part of which you could spend on a well-deserved vacation next year.

A little more research convinced me that for $3,000, a couple could enjoy a week at an all-inclusive resort in Mexico, go sightseeing in

London or explore Thailand. Yes, you could spend more. And, if you have kids, you may need to pick a vacation within driving distance.

Here's the challenge: Plan ahead, save for, and go on vacation over Labor Day weekend in 2019.

Plan

This is the fun part, and it's free. Go online, browse travel books at a bookstore, or visit the library. Where have you always wanted to visit? What have you wanted to do but have never done?

Make the plan real by picking your travel dates and creating a travel budget for:

- Transportation
- Lodging
- Food
- Activities

Save

Sticking with our $3,000 vacation next Labor Day means you'll need to save $250 each month to arrive home without any credit card debt.

You can do this by reducing your spending on groceries, eating out, and entertainment. Using the Bureau of Labor Statistics averages above, we need to cut all spending equally by 30 percent or dramatically reduce eating out and entertainment. Your choice.

Here are 10 ideas for cutting back so you can go on vacation.

1. Skip the coffee shop and drinks with your meal.

2. Share an entree.

3. Bring your lunch to work four out of five days each week.

4. Go on a picnic instead of eating out.

5. On the weekend, cook for the week ahead.

6. Skip the movie theater.

7. Make your gear last another season.

8. Enjoy a free event or concert.

9. Go for a hike.

10. Use the library for books, movies, and audio books.

If you find that the vacation you've planned will cost more than you can afford to spend, scale back by:

- Reducing the number of days.
- Choosing a less expensive place to stay for part or all of your vacation.
- Limiting the number of excursions and activities.
- Changing your travel dates and going in the offseason when you're more likely to get a deal.

I was planning on going out to eat after finishing my column, but now I'm going to cook at home so I can go on vacation.

51

ELIMINATE FINANCIAL RISK AND REAP THE REWARDS

My family and I play board and card games at breakfast. Yes, maybe a little strange, but it's the one meal we can count on having as a family.

Win or lose; I love playing games, especially ones that involve risks and rewards. They create twists, turns, and surprising outcomes that make me laugh.

Little did I know, these games would hold valuable lessons about personal finance. They have reminded me that all choices involve risk. I think failing to acknowledge risk is the cause of most personal finance problems.

Just by living, we take financial risks. Cars break down and need to be repaired. Houses need maintenance — household items and technology break and need to be replaced. Money is borrowed and needs to be repaid.

Financial risks add up. The more risks we take, the more likely things are to go wrong, and the more we need to spend to get ourselves back to where we started. All of this spending can leave your bank account depleted if you haven't built up a cushion to weather the setbacks.

How much risk are you taking? Let's find out. Give yourself one point for each of the following:

- Each credit card you have. ___
- Each car you own. ___
- Each home you own. ___
- Each boat, motorcycle and ATV you own. ___
- Each television, cellphone, tablet, and computer you own. ___

Give yourself two points for each of these:

- Each personal loan and credit card balance. ___
- Each mortgage and home equity loan. ___
- Each auto, boat, motorcycle, and ATV loan. ___
- Each job you have. ___
- Each child you have. ___

Subtract one point for each:

- A written monthly budget that you follow and regularly revise. ___

- Money accumulated for purchases made less than monthly. ___

- Medical insurance, short-term disability insurance, long-term disability insurance, and life insurance. ____

- An emergency fund equal to at least three months of living expenses. ____

- Spending less than 35 percent of your take-home pay on housing (rent, mortgage, property taxes, homeowners' association fees). ____

- Investing 15 percent of your take-home pay. ____

Add up your point total to see where you rank. If your risk level is higher than you'd like, you'll know where you can make changes to reduce that risk.

- 20 or more points: Your financial risk is very high. It's time to take action to reduce that risk and reset your course.

- 16-20 points: Your financial risk level is moderate to high. With a series of changes, financial security can be yours.

- 10-15 points: Your financial risk level is moderate to low. Just a few changes will give you financial security.

- 0-9 points: Your financial risk level is very low. Congratulations, you have true financial security.

52

MONEY ADVICE I'D LEAVE TO MY GRANDKIDS

We are living in the gig economy. Many of us work part-time or on projects, provide a service or own a small business. Each of these is temporary, but they shape who we are. Writing Money Savvy has transformed me.

It has been one of my gigs since November 2009. After more than 100 columns, today is the final one that will run in *The Durango Herald*. I am deeply grateful to the staff, management, and owners of the *Herald* for the opportunity and support.

And I appreciate you. Each reader who has shared their story with me posted a column on their refrigerator, or passed one along to someone they care about has given me confidence.

Being dyslexic, I grew up believing that I was stupid. This chipped away at my confidence. Since my 20s, I'd said, "I want to be a writer." But I didn't believe in myself enough to write. When I discovered my passion for helping people take control of their money so they can live the life of their dreams, I wanted to share what I was learning with as many people as possible.

Money Savvy was born out of my passion for helping. I'd never even written for a school newspaper, but I proposed the idea of a regular personal finance column to the *Herald*. Now, I dare to call myself a writer. Thank you for reading.

I'll leave you with this list of the 10 things to take control of your money and live the life of your dreams.

1. Budget monthly for:

   - Basic necessities.
   - Debts and obligations.
   - Less-than-monthly expenses.
   - Nice-to-have items and small luxuries.

2. Build an emergency fund.

   - Start with $1,000.
   - When all non-mortgage debts are paid off, grow it to equal three to six months of living expenses.

3. List all of your debts and pay them off ASAP by:

   - Focusing all of your payoff effort on the smallest debt.
   - Paying the minimum required payments on all other debts.
   - Setting a goal of paying off all non-mortgage debt within 18 months.

4. Limit your housing costs.

   - Set a target of not more than 25 percent of your income.
   - When borrowing, use a 15-year mortgage.

5. Control your lifestyle.

   - When you get a raise, add just 25 percent of it to your spending.
   - Invest the rest for financial security.
   - Invest for 25 years.
   - Automatically invest 25 percent of your income.

6. Use low-cost, diversified mutual funds.

7. Dream! Live your bucket list regularly:

   - Pick a dream from your list.
   - Create a budget for your goal.
   - Decide by when you want to achieve it.
   - Divide the money budgeted by the number of months until you need the money.
   - Decide where the money will come from to save for your dream. If it seems like too much money for you to save each month, reduce your budget and/or lengthen the amount of time to save.

8. Give your time and talents to living a fulfilled life.

9. Be part of a mutually supportive community that will:

- Challenge you to grow.

- Confront your self-imposed limits.

10. Be an active member of a circle of support to:

- Be accountable.

- Overcome obstacles to your goals

- Celebrate what's working in your life and examine what's not.

It is said, "What we seek to give to others is what we need most." Thank you for playing a part in helping me to live the life of my dreams.

You can continue to find my writing at www.personalfinancecoaching.com and sign up for my email newsletter there, too.

ABOUT:

MATT KELLY

Matt is the author of the newspaper column *Money Savvy*, a certified full leader for the New Warrior Training Adventure, a leadership trainer for the ManKind Project, a personal finance coach, and a certified Book Yourself Solid coach.

Matt is a graduate of Michael Port's *Heroic Public Speaking* and is a sought after speaker and media source for personal finance, leadership, and living your purpose.

He lives in Portland, Oregon with his wife, Cheri, their dog Lulu, and Misha the cat.

161

www.ingramcontent.com/pod-product-compliance
Lightning Source LLC
Chambersburg PA
CBHW022039190326
41520CB00008B/642